EUROPEAN WORKS COUNCILS

Book One

The Establishment of European Works Councils
From information committee to social actor
Wolfgang Lecher, Bernhard Nagel, Hans-Wolfgang Platzer
ISBN 1 84014 886 1

European Works Councils
Developments, types and networking

WOLFGANG LECHER
Hans-Böckler Foundation, Düsseldorf

HANS-WOLFGANG PLATZER
University of Applied Sciences, Fulda

STEFAN RÜB
University of Applied Sciences, Fulda

KLAUS-PETER WEINER
University of Applied Sciences, Fulda

Translated by Pete Burgess

Routledge
Taylor & Francis Group

LONDON AND NEW YORK

First published 2001 by Gower Publishing

Reissued 2018 by Routledge
2 Park Square, Milton Park, Abingdon, Oxon OX14 4RN
711 Third Avenue, New York, NY 10017, USA

Routledge is an imprint of the Taylor & Francis Group, an informa business

Publisher's Note
The publisher has gone to great lengths to ensure the quality of this reprint but
points out that some imperfections in the original copies may be apparent.

Disclaimer
The publisher has made every effort to trace copyright holders and welcomes
correspondence from those they have been unable to contact.

A Library of Congress record exists under LC control number: 2001087141

ISBN 13: 978-1-138-70268-4 (hbk)
ISBN 13: 978-1-138-70269-1 (pbk)
ISBN 13: 978-1-315-20353-9 (ebk)

Contents

Abbreviations

ACME	Association des Assureurs Coopératifs et Mutualistes Européens (European Mutual and Co-operative Insurance Association)
BIPAR	Bureau International des Producteurs d'Assurances et des Réassurances (International Federation of Insurance Intermediaries)
CEA	Comité Européen des Assurances (European Insurance Committee)
CEC	Commission of the European Communities
CEEP	European Centre of Enterprises with Public Participation and Enterprises of General Economic Interest
CFDT	Confédération Française Démocratique de Travail (Democratic French Confederation of Labour)
DAG	Deutsche Angestellten-Gewerkschaft (German Salaried Employees Union
DGB	Deutscher Gewerkschaftsbund (German Trade Union Confederation)
ECF-IUF	European Committee of Food, Catering and Allied Workers within the IUF (see below)
EEA	European Economic Area
EMF	European Metalworkers Federation
EMU	Economic and Monetary Union
ETUC	European Trades Union Confederation
ETUI	European Trade Union Institute
EU	European Union
Euro-FIET	European section of the International Federation of Commercial, Clercial, Professional, and Technical Employees FIET (now part of Uni-Europa)
EWC	European Works Council

FB-UE	Fédération Bancaire de l'Union Européene
FIET	International Federation of Commercial, Clerical, Professional, and Technical Employees (now part of Union Network International)
HBV	Gewerkschaft Handel, Banken und Versicherungen (German Commerce, Bank and Insurance Trade Union)
HOTREC	Confederation of National Associations of Hotels, Restaurants, Cafés and Similar Establishments in the EU and EEA
IUF	International Union of Foodworkers
MSF	Manufacturing, Science, Finance Trade Union (UK)
NGG	Gewerkschaft Nahrung-Genuss-Gaststätte (Trade Union of Catering and Allied Workers) (D)
SETCa	Trade Union of Employees, Technicans and Managerial Staffs (B)
SNB	Special Negotiating Body
UNICE	Union of Industrial and Employers' Confederations of Europe
VDU	Visual display unit
Ver.di	Vereinigte Dienstleistungsgewerkschaft (United Services Trade Union) (D)

Preface

This study of the development and networking of European Works Councils (EWCs) presents the results of a research project conducted between November 1997 and November 1998 at the University for Applied Sciences, Fulda in co-operation with the Economic and Social Science Institute (WSI) of the Hans Böckler Foundation, Düsseldorf.

Based on a qualitative and comparative case-study analysis of five EWCs in each of three sectors – banking, insurance and the food industry – together with an analysis of the sectoral preconditions and prospects for their networking, the study pursues a twofold objective.

Firstly, it sets out to make a contribution to basic empirical research in the still widely unexplored field of the Europeanisation of industrial relations, the shape and co-ordinates of which are, and will be, critically influenced by the development of EWCs. It follows on, using a wider analytical framework, from the study of the establishment of EWCs in the chemical and engineering industries in four countries published in Lecher, Nagel, Platzer et al. (*The Establishment of European Works Councils*, Ashgate, 1999).

Secondly, by adopting an approach which lies at the intersection of comparative industrial relations research and integration theory, it aims to capture the empirical diversity of the development of EWCs by means of a typology and to analyse the links between the transnational enterprise-level of the EWC, the meso-level of the branch and the macro-level of European trade union and employer organisations in terms of current and possible future processes of networking.

Acknowledgments

This study would not have been possible without the generous willingness of very many representatives of EWCs, of national and European trade unions, and of EU institutions to provide us with detailed, relevant and frank information, either in interviews or as participants in the project's review conferences. We gratefully acknowledge their cooperation.

The review conferences were made possible by the financial support of the European Commission, DG V, and the financial and organisational assistance of the Brussels office of the Friedrich Ebert Foundation.

Finally, we are especially indebted to the Hans Böckler Foundation for its financial support for both the research project and the English translation.

Wolfgang Lecher, Hans-Wolfgang Platzer,
Stefan Rüb, Klaus-Peter Weiner

Acknowledgements

1 Introduction

Two central themes overshadow current debate – both academic and political – on the future of industrial relations in Europe: economic globalisation and the advancing process of European economic and political integration.

Indeed European integration, which through the Single Market project of the 1980s and Economic and Monetary Union (EMU) in the 1990s has been driven forward primarily in economic terms, is itself both a consequence and expression of economic internationalisation (Schirm, 1997). The creation of a transnational economic and monetary space is leading to a 'debordering' of national policies, accompanied by a transformation in the structure and forms of 'governance within the dynamic multi-level system of the European Union' (Jachtenfuchs and Kohler-Koch, 1996).

The main questions raised by these developments are:

- To what extent are the social and welfare-state structures of the EU's Member States and their national systems of industrial relations affected by this new environment – and how are they changing?
- How can social and employment policies and approaches to collective bargaining be structured in a 'post-national constellation' (Habermas, 1998)?
- What scope will remain for national social and political institutions – and the national protagonists in collective bargaining? And under what conditions can national actors retain or regain their capacity to shape and direct policies and processes at national level?
- What will be the significance of the supra-national European level and what powers and democratic procedures need to be established at European level to ensure that it can contribute to political and economic governance and the solution of social and economic problems?
- And finally, under what conditions, in what form, and with what dynamic and scale might cross-border and supra-national arenas of industrial relations emerge (Platzer, 1998a; 1998b)?

Needless to say, these questions have prompted a wealth of divergent analyses and prognoses. The present study, with its specific focus on Euro-

1

pean Works Councils (EWCs), also takes these interrelated sets of problems and developments as its starting point.

Aims of the Study

This study sets out to offer a contribution to the debate on the transformation and development of industrial relations within the transnational economy and multi-level political system of the European Union. In particular, it seeks to draw out the complexities of processes of Europeanisation in the sphere of industrial relations by locating itself at the point of intersection between comparative industrial relations and integration theory. Its object – the European Works Council (EWC) – is an exemplar of an institution which is situated at the interface between these two fields, in terms both of the preconditions for and prospects of its development.

The study analyses the development of EWCs in the banking, insurance and food industries by means of a cross-country comparison. It describes and explains how EWCs are constituted and develop, investigates the scope for EWCs within the new European-transnational structure of enterprise-based industrial relations and explores how this scope has been exploited. At the same time, it also looks beyond individual enterprises and EWCs and considers the needs, possibilities and prospects for linking EWCs into wider networks. The guiding supposition here is that networking processes amongst EWCs in individual branches, or between these and national and European-level trade unions, are not only now possible in principle, given the stage of development reached by EWCs, but would also be a logical strategic step.

Building networks can serve a variety of aims and objectives. In the first place, networks might help consolidate and develop EWCs themselves, for example by disseminating 'best practice'. At the same time, networks also point beyond the level of the transnational enterprise inasmuch as the resources that EWC networks might be able to mobilise and transmit, such as improved information and an enhanced capacity to act beyond the national level, could constitute a force pressing for social and employment regulation, and collective bargaining, at European level.

Whether and to what extent such 'bottom up' processes will prevail – that is, whether EWCs can form an enterprise-based substructure for a system of transnational industrial relations arenas at meso- and macro-level – will depend on a number of factors.

One primary consideration is how EWCs themselves will continue to develop – a process with both qualitative and quantitative dimensions. On the quantitative side, what will be decisive is whether EWCs will become established on a truly 'extensive' basis. An estimated 1,800 multi-national businesses meet the requirements of the European Works Directive. By late-1996 some 460 EWCs had been established under the provisions of Article 13 of the Directive which allowed for the conclusion of 'voluntary' agreements. A further 170 had been established by May 2000 under Article 6 of the Directive which requires compliance with a formalised procedure both on negotiations on an EWC agreement and delegation or election to the EWC itself, depending on how the Directive has been transposed into national law. Although those EWCs so far been established have mainly been in companies with large workforces and considerable economic impact, there remains an evident gulf between the number of EWCs established and the Directive's theoretical coverage. The qualitative question is whether and how EWCs will advance from the status of forums for the receipt of information disclosed by management to effective transnational actors, capable of actively representing employee interests.

A second critical issue is the current state and future development of the organisation and policies of European-level trade union and employer organisations, both at branch-level (European industry federations) and 'peak' level (ETUC and UNICE). The institutionalised scope for 'sectoral' and 'multi-sectoral' dialogue created by the Maastricht Treaty offers a number of points at which closer interaction within and between the social partners and parties to collective bargaining at European level might begin to crystallise. The Treaty, for example, created structures for dealing with employment issues at the meso-level of the branch and the macro-level of multi-sectoral social dialogue and specified the issues on which European regulations may be concluded. Such regulations could, in turn, promote the development of EWCs and their capacity and strategic approach in a 'top down' process.

Above and beyond this, Economic and Monetary Union (EMU) has transformed the conditions for competition and economic management in Europe, with implications for all levels of industrial relations and collective bargaining in the Member States. It poses fresh challenges and places new demands on national, and especially transnational, systems of employment regulation and collective bargaining.

A plethora of interactions and feedback mechanisms link the quantitative and qualitative development of EWCs, on the one hand, and multi-sectoral European developments in the sphere of social dialogue and negotiation on the other. This study will seek to unravel these interconnections and explore their potential for development.

Networks, it is argued here, can perform a variety of 'bridging functions' between the transnational enterprise- and workplace-level and the European-sectoral level of trade union policy and employment regulation: these embrace institutional structures, the circulation of information, and policy. By analysing the developmental dynamic of these dimensions and their interaction we hope to offer a basis for assessing whether industrial relations will become Europeanised, for exploring how such a process might take place, and for identifying the structures, forms and characteristic features of cross-border and supra-national industrial relations.

Specifically, this will entail the following:

- Using qualitative survey methods, we analyse the development of EWCs in five transnational companies in each of three branches (banking, insurance and food). These 15 case-studies are intended to contribute to both deepening and broadening the stock of knowledge in what is a new research field dedicated to a novel institution.

- These findings on the developmental dynamic of and prospects for EWCs, together with the results of previous research (Lecher et.al., 1999), which analysed eight EWCs in the chemical and engineering industries, make up the empirical basis for a proposed typology of EWCs. This typology is intended to facilitate some initial generalisations about EWCs and enable additional hypotheses to be made. Moreover, by offering a descriptive and explanatory model of EWCs that takes account of their diversity and is rooted in a systematic presentation of their origins, we hope to be able to shed some light on the controversial issue of the 'Europeanisation' of industrial relations – in this case at enterprise and establishment level.

- The study will then seek to establish whether and to what extent EWCs – that is, the actors at enterprise/workplace level – and national and European trade unions are beginning to express a need for EWCs to be networked, if they have any thoughts on how this might be achieved, and what steps have been taken towards implementing it. This will be pursued on the basis of the following working hypothesis: just as the EWC is a 'test case' for a European mode of regulation of industrial relations at enterprise level based on the provision of procedures and options, the presuppositions and prospects for networking EWCs are also an entirely open matter. Creating networks is one choice in the broader process through which enterprise-level and trade union actors search out and identify options in what is still a complex and at times opaque transnational terrain. This part of the study will initially set out

to ascertain the need for and perceptions of capacity building at trans-enterprise and transnational level and to explore organisational initiatives in, and possible barriers to, the development of such networks.
• Based on these experiences, the study will conclude with a discussion of the paths along which transnational industrial relations might develop. The challenges associated with this question – in the context of economic internationalisation and the economic and political integration of Europe – are of central importance both for policy development in the broadest sense, and trade union strategy in particular. The initial task here is to find a suitable analytical framework for dealing with the multi-level processes of the Europeanisation of industrial relations, which we pursue via a critical review of recent approaches in European integration studies and comparative industrial relations.

Analytical Framework

The concepts of 'Europeanisation' and 'European industrial relations' are understood in widely differing ways in the literature. The main areas of controversy are, firstly, the choice of indicators for measuring the 'Europeanisation' of industrial relations and, secondly, the identification of a reference model against which the development of cross-border and supra-national industrial relations might be gauged.

The classic approaches adopted by comparative industrial relations are strongly rooted in the 'convergence-divergence' paradigm in which 'Europeanisation' is measured in terms of whether and to what extent the economic and political process of establishing an international community – in its specific EU form – generates the same or comparable processes of adaptation seen in the industrial relations systems of the Member States. Should a convergent pattern be identified which differs significantly from the developmental path of other industrialised countries – such as those Western Europe countries which were outside the EU at least until the mid-1990s – then 'Europeanisation' may be said to be taking place. Comparative studies have found no evidence to support a model of Europeanisation operationalised in this way (Traxler, 1995; Armingeon, 1994).

Cross-country comparison of systems of industrial relations in the EU Member States since the 1980s suggests the following:

> The transformation in industrial relations (is) characterised in its various institutional and economic-material dimensions both by convergent and divergent

developmental tendencies. However, these are only common to certain groups of countries, whose configuration varies according to field of policy and development in question. As a consequence, the overall development of national industrial relations within the framework of the EU is marked by continuing structural and institutional diversity and economic and material disparity (Platzer, 1998b, p. 257).

However, this general finding from a traditional comparativist perspective fails to capture the specific patterns of response and adjustment of industrial relations systems at national level to the process of EU integration over the past decade. One significant illustration of this is represented by the newly-forged 'Social Pacts' seen in many EU Member States (Hassel, 1998) or the revitalisation of tripartism attributable to the convergence processes triggered by Economic and Monetary Union.

Although comparative analysis and the question of convergent or divergent structural developments and paths of adjustment of national industrial relations remain relevant to the approach chosen here, the evidence of diversity in national systems of industrial relations calls for an approach to the conditions and perspectives of cross-border and supra-national industrial relations more rooted in the notion of *compatibility* (Lecher and Platzer, 1996).

In addition, the empirical diversity and evolutionary character of processes of Europeanisation observable in industrial relations, together with the transnational dynamic in the mediation of interests and interaction of the social partners at European level, require a conceptualisation of 'European industrial relations' which is both broad yet more nuanced.

This requires, firstly, deciding on the appropriate time period within which developmental stages and advances should be judged. Viewed historically, and aside from the special cases of agriculture, coal, iron and steel, up until the 1980s EC integration was characterised by a progressive integration of product markets. It was only with the project for a liberalised and deregulated internal market, initiated in the mid-1980s and largely completed by the early-1990s, that a structural and competitive framework had been created at European level with the capacity to exercise a sustained effect on the established spheres of interest, structures and traditional scope of national systems of industrial relations. The project for Economic and Monetary Union (EMU), negotiated in the Maastricht Treaty and initiated in 1993, lent further impetus to this process.

The Maastricht Treaty also extended the EU's powers in the employment and social policy field, and expanded the institutional role of the European social partners within the EU's decision-making machinery. The historical frame of reference for the process of Europeanisation in the field of industrial relations is therefore, at most, one and a half decades. This temporal frame of reference, often overlooked, is important in identifying appropriate benchmarks for the evolution of the Europeanisation of industrial relations and achieving a corresponding diachronic perspective.

Secondly, 'European industrial relations' will be understood as meaning not only or primarily the 'classical' fields of collective bargaining, through which the parties to collective bargaining or the social partners autonomously – but now at supra-national level – regulate terms and conditions of employment. Rather, it embraces:

> all forms of cross-border or supranational relationship between the social partners at the various levels at which they may exist, together with the interplay of national and EU institutions and the social partners in formulating and implementing employment and social policy (Platzer, 1998b).

Such an approach to the transformation of national and the development of transnational industrial relations within the European 'Single Integrated Space' has parallels with the recent paradigm shift in integration studies. This centres on the dissolution of the territorial ties between economic processes and problems and their treatment within the framework of a dynamic multi-level system of governance (Jachtenfuchs and Kohler-Koch, 1996). The basis for this is the observable changes in the structures, processes and contents of Member States' policies as a consequence of integration.

The concept of a 'dynamic multi-level system' proceeds on the assumption that approaches derived, often implicitly, from the model of the state are of only limited use when applied to the EU system of governance. 'Dynamic' refers to the fact that institutions and their competencies are subject to constant change. 'Multi-level' refers to the fact that the EU encompasses the Member States within an overarching system – but one in which national (or sub-national) political, social and legal systems do not cease to exist.

This change in perspective avoids the teleological bias of earlier neo-functionalist or (neo-) federalist versions of integration theory. Attention is directed to how the governance of Europe (without a central European government) and an authoritative EU allocation of resources are both possible and indeed accomplished. Although such a conceptualisation is not as demanding as that of a 'model' and does not lay claim to the status of a theory, it does open the way to the analysis of a complex decision-making structure.

This research programme contains two problem areas which are directly, and indirectly, relevant for systems of industrial relations.

The first is the issue of how procedures for democratic debate, decision-making and implementation, which are regarded as effective and legitimate at national level, are changing within the multi-level system and what impact this form of governance is having on the inclusion or exclusion of social actors and the corresponding balance of forces, for example, between the social partners.

The second is the issue of the ramifications of this system of EU governance for national social-welfare states in Western Europe – not only as one field of policy amongst many but as a system which serves to define the social order of Western European societies, at the core of which are systems of industrial relations.

The need for empirical study in this area is considerable, as is the number of unresolved theoretical and analytical issues raised by the multi-level approach. At the same time, this approach offers evident heuristic and analytical benefits. As far as the supra-national level of industrial relations is concerned, it avoids prescriptive yardsticks rooted in (national) traditions of corporatism or centralised collective bargaining and social partner organisation. (For instance, European 'big unions' will not emerge in the foreseeable future and are not the benchmark against which the efficacy of union activity in the EU should be measured.) As far as the linkages and feedback effects between national and (potential) European levels of employment regulation and collective bargaining are concerned, a multi-level approach which takes full account of the complexity of the phenomenon can also help avoid resort to zero-sum frameworks and unidirectional patterns of explanation, in which one level's gain must entail another's loss.

A multi-level approach allows the traditional comparativist perspective (convergence-divergence paradigm) to be extended and redirected. The key issue becomes that of *convergent* practices and roles and *compatible* interests and approaches on the part of industrial relations actors – at enterprise and higher levels of collective bargaining – within European frameworks and institutional contexts. In turn, this broader perspective allows indicators for the Europeanisation of industrial relations and the features of a developing European multi-level system of industrial relations to be proposed and tested. For example:

1) Europeanisation of policy and interest articulation at national level on the part of the parties to collective bargaining can be said to be in train when the economic and political framework set by the EU significantly impinges on or alters the definition and perception of interests and the forms in which issues are tackled. Such processes of Europeanisation at

national level constitute the foundation of, and are usually accompanied by, the creation and extension of cross-border networks of formal and informal communication, co-operation and co-ordination.

2) 'Europeanisation' of industrial relations will become defined via a second characteristic – namely, an EU-specific pattern of transnationalisation – to the extent that vertical (cross-level) and horizontal (cross-border) networks act to reinforce each other at the various levels of employment regulation within the EU's 'Single Integrated Space' and then differentiate themselves from other relationships between labour market actors at international and global level.

3) A genuinely European regime of supra-national industrial relations could be said to exist if mechanisms for regulating conflicts over bargaining issues emerge and become sufficiently consolidated at European-transnational level to influence, transform or possibly even replace national arrangements on a sustained basis (Platzer, 1998b).

Viewed in evolutionary terms, the criteria and process features (1) and (2) characterise developments since the mid-1980s. The process elements of (3) are – as yet – only rudimentary. Whether and to what extent changed framework conditions, such as the impact of EMU, will promote the trans- and supranational path of development cannot yet be reliably predicted. This study of the Europeanisation of industrial relations is located within this broader context of the debate around European integration. Its conceptual approach – a typology of EWCs and the prospects for their networking – reflects the multi-level approach to processes of Europeanisation and seeks to contribute to the analysis of the preconditions, scope and prospects for cross-border and supra-national industrial relations in Europe.

Approach, Course and Method of Research

This study is based on an approach which combines elements both of basic and applied research. It analyses the development of EWCs, and the prospects for networking between them, by means of a multi-country comparison across three branches of the economy: food, banking, and insurance.

The dual aim of the project – to carry out EWC case-studies together with sectoral comparisons of networking between EWCs – is part of a broader research programme. Our previous study (Lecher et.al., 1999) analysed the establishment and constitution of EWCs in the metalworking and chemical industries. This project looks at three new sectors, two of them in services. This extension of the empirical basis of our research has allowed us to develop a typology of EWCs and offer some initial explanatory hypotheses: these are set out in Chap. 3 below.

Whilst the previous study was primarily concerned with a *cross-country* comparison of EWC developments (two companies in German, France, Italy, and the UK and the relationship between parent-company and subsidiary), the main focus in the present study is the *branch* (see Chap. 2.4). This allows a more detailed study of the branch-specific conditions relevant to the process of EWC development, including the differing preconditions set for companies and trade unions. It also serves to structure the field in sectoral terms – the level at which demands are likely to be placed on EWCs to take action above the level of the individual enterprise and at which EWCs networks seem most likely to emerge.

The sample of five EWCs examined in each sector encompasses:

- Parent companies in the food sector from the UK (2), France, Germany and Switzerland.
- Parent companies in banking from the Netherlands, Belgium, France and Germany (2).
- Parent companies in insurance from France, Belgium, Germany (2) and Switzerland.

Data collection was based on a combination of secondary data analysis and structured interviews and conferences ('triangulation'). It entailed the following successive stages.

- Secondary data analysis served to establish the profiles of the EWCs (origin, date of agreement etc.) of the corresponding undertaking (basic data, structure, strategy) as well as the respective branch (size composition of companies, degree of concentration, product characteristics, level of internationalisation, EU regulatory framework, industrial relations at meso-level).
- In a second stage, interviews were conducted with one representative of each of the EWCs (usually members of the select committee, the chair or deputy chair) of the relevant German and European trade union.
- Based on this empirical foundation, in a final stage a two-day conference was held in Brussels for each branch to which representatives of the EWCs in the study and their respective national and European trade

unions were invited. These conferences had a dual function. The first was to review, extend and deepen the material collected in the earlier stages. The second was to mirror the self-reflexive and practical dimension of the research: that is, to create constellations of actors as it were 'en miniature' and indicate areas for sharing experiences and possible joint action which might serve to initiate networking.

All three conferences were organised using the same schema and form in order to allow comparison between the findings. The participating EWC representatives (including on some occasions representatives from subsidiaries) and the representatives of each of the national trade unions and European trade union organisations acted as 'experts in their own cause'. The discussion was organised into three sessions and structured so that actual experience as well as perceived needs and prospects could be exchanged. One session was devoted to the structure, working methods and development of the EWC; a second to the current and potential fields of activity of EWCs and the typical patterns for a supra-enterprise, branch-based problem solving; and a third to the structural and organisational issues of cross-company communication, co-operation and networking.

In addition to their practical role, these conferences also had a methodological aim and analytical meaning in that they 'simulated' a situation which is typical of the current stage of the development of EWCs and how they are integrated with the initial steps towards sectoral level European industrial relations – namely, the difficult task of finding a strategic approach and creating institutional stability within a new transnational terrain.

The results which this process yielded offer a realistic picture of the complexities of Europeanisation. At the same time, they also present a number of starting points – each with its own Utopian component – for reflections on possible developmental paths for a European industrial relations.

However, the study does not provide a detailed presentation of the empirical findings on a case-by-case basis. Rather, it aims to direct attention to the generic issues raised by confining itself to the main features of the case studies and by using a typology to examine actual and potential networks.

2 European Works Councils in the Context of European Industrial Relations

The Establishment and Dynamic of European Works Councils

The adoption of the Directive on the establishment of European Works Councils (EWCs) in multinational enterprises on 22 September 1994 can be viewed as the most significant innovation in European employment and social policy in recent years.[1] The measure is intended to ensure that employees in companies and groups of companies with operations in a number of Member States of the European Economic Area (EEA)[2] have rights to information and consultation with their employer. The Directive, which embraces some 1,800 companies headquartered both within and outside the EU with a total of some 15 million employees, has been transposed into national law in virtually all Member States or become the object of a national-level collective agreement – albeit in some cases some time after the deadline date of 22 September 1996.[3] After many years of debate and controversy for the first time in the history of the process of European integration the EWC Directive created the political and legal foundations for employee involvement in multinational companies. The key steps towards the establishment of EWCs had already been taken in the 1980s with the voluntary establishment of a number of 'European Information Committees' in large French multinational groups. The Directive allowed for a two-year period following its adoption during which employers and employee representatives could establish EWCs on a 'voluntary' basis, without the formal negotiating procedures set out in Articles 5/6 of the Directive, provided some minimum conditions were met on coverage of the agreement. By September 1996 around 460 voluntary agreements had been concluded on the legal basis of Article 13 of the EWC Directive. Since then an estimated further 170 agreements have been negotiated under Article 6 of the Directive.

In comparison with the national provisions in most EU Member States, the Directive defines information and consultation quite tightly. Although employers and employee representatives may choose to specify the issues and procedures for the EWC in their undertaking, the Directive sets out a number of minimum provisions ('Subsidiary Requirements') in an Annex which can be triggered should the parties fail to come an agreement. According to the definition in the subsidiary requirements, the information which managements must disclose to employees encompasses:

> the progress of the business of the Community-scale undertaking or Community-scale group of undertakings and its prospects.

This includes, in particular:

> the structure, economic and financial situation, the probable development of the business and of production and sales, the situation and probable trend of employment, investments, and substantial changes concerning organisation, introduction new working methods or production processes, transfers of production, mergers, cut-backs or closures of undertakings, establishments or important parts thereof, and collective redundancies.

In addition, the EWC must also be informed and consulted in the event of 'exceptional circumstances affecting the employees' interests to a considerable extent'.

To quote one commentator, in adopting the Directive the EU Council of Ministers 'initially restricted itself to the more slender branch of the practice of employee participation in Europe – namely information and consultation' (Höland, 1997, p. 60). Participation under the Directive only entails a right of involvement, not of co-determination. As a consequence, although employee representatives may be included in the process by which companies make decisions, they have no right of veto. In addition, the Directive makes no provision for measures which are subject to information and consultation to be delayed until after the procedure has been completed. Reactions in the case of Renault, in which group management did not inform the EWC 'in good time' about the impending closure of the company's plant at Vilvoorde in Belgium, highlighted the controversy surrounding the issue of the timeliness of information and consultation. A number – albeit limited – of EWC agreements have made express reference to when information must be provided. Moreover, initial research into the practice of EWCs shows that employee representatives want to move beyond the framework of participation provided by the Directive, or have already done so; in some cases this has been carried out via formal agreements with group managements (Lecher et. al., 1999).

The Directive embodies a consistent realisation of the – still controversial – principle of subsidiarity included in the Maastricht Treaty. The Directive regulates the right to information and consultation solely at the European level, a level not amenable to regulation by individual EU Member States. The original proposals also included minimum standards for information and consultation at national-level. These were not contained in the final draft but instead were proposed in a separate instrument put forward in late-1998.[4] Moreover, the Directive did not seek to harmonise national provisions. National legal requirements or established custom and practice were not only left untouched but were seen as a diverse foundation for the application of the Directive, which complements them with a European dimension. Although subsidiarity has enabled governments of Member States, together with national trade unions with their differing structures, strategies and programmes, to accept the Directive, the relationship with national regulations and procedures has also thrown up a number of problems with implications for the practical operation of EWCs. For example, employee representatives on an EWC or Special Negotiating Body – now mandatory with the expiry of the possibility of voluntary agreements – 'can be dependent on different sources of legitimacy, depending on their national origins, and do not all enjoy the same degree of protection' (Rademacher, 1996, p. 184).

Subsidiarity also means that realising the aims of the Directive is initially a matter for employees and group managements. The form, composition and powers, procedures, operation, structure and resources of EWCs can be agreed between them in a practical acknowledgement of their autonomy. This is intended to facilitate flexible solutions, tailored to differing corporate realities. Whilst the procedure for reaching agreement could be freely chosen prior to the transposition deadline of September 1996 (or December 1999 in the UK), the establishment of an EWC is now prescribed by the Directive. Should the employee side submit an application, a Special Negotiating Body (SNB) must be set up to represent the employees in the undertaking and conduct negotiations with group management. Only if these negotiations prove fruitless – and after a prescribed lapse of time – can an EWC be established in accordance with the Directive's minimum fallback provisions, the 'Subsidiary Requirements'. The parties can also agree not to establish an EWC. Again, this aspect of subsidiarity in the Directive went a long way to meet the call from the employer side for a high degree of voluntarism to be included in the provisions.

The inclusion of the principle of subsidiarity in the Directive suggests that this might be seen as an indication of a paradigm shift in the regulatory approach of the Commission, with a preference for 'soft' over 'hard' regulation (Streeck and Vitols, 1993). On this analysis, EWCs would be the product of diverse – and largely non-mandatory – regulatory policies, legal systems, industrial relations practices, trade union strategies and corporate power structures. This contrasts with the more ambitious reading of these developments, according to which the establishment and development of EWCs is an expression of processes of social, economic and political transnationalisation, which – although having national origins and points of reference – none the less constitute a new and developing dimension within the framework of a complex and dynamic European multi-level system of industrial relations (Platzer, 1998b). The basis for this approach can be found in a historical reconstruction of how EWCs came to be established (Platzer and Weiner, 1998). This indicates a strong and mutually-reinforcing interaction between the establishment of European information bodies on a voluntary basis and the adoption and implementation of the Directive. Whilst without the 'voluntaristic pioneer projects' it would have been impossible to build up the trade union and political pressure needed to have the Directive adopted, in turn without the Directive it would not have been possible to negotiate as many EWCs as have been agreed, given the opposition of many managements. The practical operation of EWCs under voluntary agreements also anticipated and ultimately facilitated the procedural requirements of the Directive by prefiguring its legal norms, just as these in turn influenced the practice of EWCs – evidenced, for example, in the renegotiation of several agreements which had been concluded prior to the adoption of the Directive in 1994.

The process of the establishment and development of EWCs can be divided into three phases. The first, the 'pioneer phase' of voluntary agreements, led on to a phase in which agreements were voluntarily concluded, but against the background of Article 13 of the Directive. This was followed by the current phase, under which employers are obliged to establish EWCs if employee representatives wish it, using the procedures set out in Articles 5 and 6 of the Directive. The pioneer phase saw a number of initiatives which played a crucial role in subsequent developments. These included the presentation of the draft Directive in December 1990 by the Commission and the creation of EU budget line 4004/3 to facilitate international meetings at the instigation of the European Parliament and Commission following a campaign by European trade unions. This allowed a number of direct meetings between workforces and trade union representatives at European companies. In this sense, the negotiation and establishment of voluntarily agreed EWCs had already taken place 'in the shadow of the law'. During this phase some 40 EWCs were established, of which fewer than a quarter were set up in the initial period prior to the early-1990s. During the period of 'Directive-driven'

EWC agreements, which extended from the adoption of the Directive up until the September 1996 transposition deadline, this number increased tenfold. The number of agreements concluded under the procedures of Articles 5/6 of the Directive could ultimately triple or quadruple this total, based on assessments of the number of companies within the scope of the Directive.

The first pilot projects were undertaken in the French undertakings Thomson Grand Public (1985), Bull (1988) and Rhône Poulenc (1990). That this was so is primarily attributable to factors located in the politics and structures of the French system of industrial relations. Firstly, the 1982 'Auroux' laws required 'group committees' (*'comités de group'*) to be established in large undertakings. Their structure and operation established a pattern on which the later European bodies were modelled. Secondly, the first European information bodies were established in public or nationalised undertakings. And thirdly, European information committees also corresponded with new management approaches, the aim of which was 'to use European agreements and structures of dialogue to promote a common awareness of problems and a European "corporate identity" amongst employees and their trade union representatives' (Rehfeldt, 1994, p. 290). In contrast, the interest of the French trade unions in concluding voluntary agreements on European company committees was the product of employer resistance to European legislation. The objective was to use voluntary agreements to create precedents for establishing workplace and trade union transnational communication and co-operation over the medium and longer term.

The European-level trade unions have been heavily involved in the EWC process, both in terms of overall political approach as well practical operation. Of the industry-level European industry federations, the European Metalworkers Federation (EMF) has been notable in its innovative and pioneering role (Platzer, 1991, p. 117). The involvement of trade unions reflects a set of particular historical experiences, organisational interests and developments in their approaches to European issues. One important experience was the widespread failure of autonomous trade union initiatives to establish world company councils in multinational concerns in the 1960s and 1970s. As a result, efforts were directed at setting up European industrial relations arrangements at group level on a regional, rather than a global, basis using concrete projects to strengthen and develop the European organisational level. Finally, the pursuit of a 'voluntaristic strategy', which characterised the pioneer phase of EWCs, was a reaction to the years of stagnation in the social policy field, but one which corresponded to the paradigm shift in political and economic management which prevailed in the early 1980s and which was manifested at European level in the Single Market project.

In the subsequent phase of support by the EU, in both institutional and financial terms, there was a marked increase in the pace at which EWCs were established. The trade unions pursued a dual-track strategy which, through the interplay of the national and European level, aimed at promoting further EWC agreements in order to create pressure for the legal regulation for which they were calling. This approach could draw support from the 'embarkation towards a social dimension to the internal market' (Däubler, 1997, p. 102) called for by the Commission and the Centre-Left majority of the European Parliament and expressed in the 1990 draft EWC Directive. Financial support from the EU allowed hundreds of European works council meetings to take place, most of which were under the aegis of the European trade union federations. They were aimed at creating the preconditions for subsequent voluntary negotiations by initiating transnational communication between workforce and trade union representatives.

The Commission's draft Directive reflected a fundamental shift in the approach to regulation from the prescription of outcomes to the creation of procedures and options through European framework legislation. In contrast to previous initiatives, 'as good as nothing was regulated. The provisions were intended to create a legal and financial basis for community-wide forms of co-operation and to facilitate "flexible and practicable" representation in the form of EWCs or decentralised "procedures for employee information and consultation" in as company-specific a way as possible' (Keller, 1996, p. 472). However, the 'subsidiary requirements' laid out in an Annex to the Directive did draw together a number of minimum provisions which began to have an impact even before the Directive had been adopted or transposed into national law. For example, some voluntary EWC agreements made explicit reference to the draft Directive. The combined effect of these factors explains the growth of EWCs, by number, branch and national HQ of parent companies during the second period of the pioneer phase.

Given the enduring opposition of national European employer associations and some governments (primarily in the UK) to any statutory provision on EWCs, a change in the political and legal context was required – as evidenced in the Maastricht Treaty and its provisions for qualified majority voting on a number of social issues (and the UK's consequent opt out which removed the main source of opposition within the Council of Ministers, thereby hastening what the veto had intended to forestall). The adoption of the EWC Directive which this change brought about led to a further spurt in the conclusion of EWC agreements. Critical in the negotiation of EWCs during this period was the pressure from and requirements of the Directive. One of the first aspects of the 'new style of politics' (Falkner, 1996) created by the new treaty provisions, which emerged even before the adoption of the Directive, was the 'enforced willingness' of the employers to negotiate on the establishment of information and consultation bodies under the new Social Dialogue procedures in view of the threat of legislation. The phase of 'enforced voluntarism' which followed the adoption of the Directive after the breakdown of these negotiations was paralleled by intensive and systematic efforts by national and European trade unions to support negotiations and characterised by the nationally diverse processes of negotiating and shaping EWCs set in train by the transposition of the Directive into national law.

Since September 1996, which marked the beginning of the phase in which EWCs became subject to the Directive, EWCs must be established via negotiations between group managements and a Special Negotiating Body (SNB), elected or delegated by workforces throughout Europe. Although in the years immediately following the phase of 'enforced voluntarism' the process of establishing EWCs stagnated, there were subsequently signs that the experiences and dynamics of EWCs voluntarily agreed before and after the Directive were beginning to influence EWCs set up under mandatory procedures. These experiences will feed into trade union and employer assessments of the Directive, pending any review. Experience of existing practice will also play a role in optimising the operation of those bodies still to be established. This confronts the trade unions in particular with a difficult challenge, if only by virtue of the sheer numbers of EWC negotiations still pending.

Regulated Diversity – EWCs as Reflected in their Agreements

By the time the period allowed under the Directive for voluntary agreements had expired, barely a third of all the companies embraced by the Directive had concluded an agreement. The degree to which the voluntary introduction of EWCs was accelerated by the gentle pressure of the law – together with the scope for employees to meet using the resources provided by budget line 4003/4 – can be seen in the large number of agreements concluded in the final twelve months before the permitted period for such agreements expired on 22 September 1996. According to a study prepared by the Dublin-based European Foundation for the Improvement of Living and Working Conditions in Europe, and based on an evaluation of 386 EWC agreements (Marginson et.al., 1998), 78 per cent of agreements were concluded in this final period. September 1996 alone, the last month in which voluntary agreements could be struck, saw the conclusion of 33 per cent of all the agreements analysed. Voluntary agreements were, therefore, not simply the precursors of the deci-

sion by the Council of Ministers (Hall, 1992; Keller, 1994) or a means of re-
fining and better substantiating the draft Directive (Marginson and Sisson,
1996, p. 183). Rather, the setting of a deadline for the conclusion of voluntary
agreements clearly served to accelerate the establishment of EWCs, and promote the introduction of EWCs on an extensive basis in European companies. In practice – as the process which led to the adoption of Directive
suggests – the 'regulatory' and 'voluntaristic' approaches are far from constituting distinct alternatives.

The Directive and its subsidiary requirements have not only had a
marked influence on the dynamic with which voluntary agreements have
been concluded, but also on the substance of such agreements. In the majority
of cases they have served as guidelines for the legitimation of the negotiating
parties and for the composition of the EWC, together with its powers and issues on which agreement has been reached. As such, the Directive and subsidiary requirements have shaped negotiations and set some limits to the
diversity of EWC structures and *modus operandi* noted above (Krieger and
Bonneton, 1995; Carley and Hall, 1996). The 1998 Dublin Foundation study
also showed that there continue to be differences between voluntary agreements as regards the type of agreement, their form and scope, the function
and powers of EWCs, their composition, the issue of the steering committee,
meetings with management, and availability of resources. These differences
are explained in the study by such factors as country of origin of the parent
company, branch, number of employees and the time when the agreement
was concluded and the influence of the trade unions (Marginson et.al., 1998).

As far as the country of origin of the company was concerned, the study
revealed considerable variation in the 'strike rate' of agreements, that is the
number of agreements as a proportion of the theoretical maximum for any
given country.[5] Whereas in France, Germany and Italy, the strike rate did not
deviate markedly from the overall average of 33 per cent, it was considerably
higher in Belgium. Three-quarters of all Belgian companies covered by the
Directive had concluded a voluntary agreement. In the Irish Republic, 60 per
cent of undertakings within the scope of the Directive had concluded a voluntary agreement. The strike rate was also above average – at 50-60 per cent
– in Finland, Sweden and Norway. It was markedly lower for undertakings
headquartered in Denmark, the Netherlands and Spain, where it was 20 per
cent or below. The same applied in Austria. In contrast, in the United King-
dom – for which the Directive did not apply in the period under consideration
– the rate was 50 per cent. More than 40 per cent of Japanese undertakings
within the scope of the Directive had also concluded a voluntary agreement,
although US companies were broadly in line with the average (ibid. pp. 12ff).

A number of factors underlay these differences including:

- the very uneven national distribution of undertakings covered by the Directive,
- the degree of internationalisation of undertakings,
- the stance adopted by group managements,
- differences in national systems of industrial relations,
- differences in systems of workplace and enterprise employee representation,
- the influence of trade unions,
- specific corporate structures and linkages.

Developments in the UK served to illustrate a specific form of European interdependence and 'transnational proliferation' of policy. Despite the UK's opt-out from the social provisions of the Maastricht Treaty, and with it the EWC Directive, and the opposition of the Conservative government and national employers' associations, voluntary agreements were concluded in a large number of British parent companies which fell under the Directive by virtue of their Mainland European and Irish workforces. Given the degree of EU economic integration and political interdependence, events in the UK can be explained by the interaction of two factors. On the one hand, there were advantages to businesses from 'going early', such as a better corporate image and the expectation that the Conservative government would be replaced; such undertakings also had to establish EWCs for their Mainland European workforces in any event. On the other, British unions were alive to the impulses emanating from Europe, as well as their transnational 'spill over' effects, and were eager to reclaim ground lost during the period of Conservative government.

The share of the overall number of agreements concluded also varied by economic sector and branch. At some 80 per cent, the proportion accounted for by manufacturing, with a further 6 per cent in other producing goods sectors, far exceeded that in services, which accounted for only 13 per cent of agreements. Metalworking alone was responsible for 35 per cent of agreements, followed by chemicals at 17 per cent. Food, drink and tobacco accounted for 12 per cent of agreements. In contrast, financial services had a share of only 5 per cent. The sectoral 'strike rate' (actual agreements as a proportion of the possible total for a sector) also varied markedly – highest in chemicals, with some 45 per cent, followed closely by food, drink and tobacco, and metalworking. Overall the 'strike rate' in manufacturing was found to be almost double the rate in services – a disparity attributable first and foremost to different levels of union organisation in these branches but also, possibly, the different approaches taken both by the companies in these sectors and the European trade union industry federations (ibid. p. 16).

There are also significant differences between EWC agreements according to the overall numbers employed in undertakings. Whereas for EU-headquartered companies, large undertakings (with more than 10,000 employees) dominated agreements concluded, with 67 per cent, in non-European companies the level was 31 per cent. In contrast, the ratio for medium-sized companies (5,000 – 10,000 employees) was more evenly balanced, at 18 per cent and 15 per cent. Substantial differences re-emerged in the case of smaller undertakings (with fewer than 5,000 employees), where European companies accounted for only 14 per cent of the European total and non-European for 54 per cent of their total (ibid. pp. 17ff). It would be reasonable to suppose that the differences between companies headquartered in Europe and those based elsewhere might be explained in terms of their respective corporate structures, and in particular by the relationship between parent companies, subsidiaries, and their respective business divisions.

In order to be able to explain the differences in voluntary agreements between countries and branches, it should be remembered that any agreement establishing an EWC needs to be judged in the context of a particular course of development. Case-studies (Lecher et.al., 1999) and reports of EWC practice (such as Deppe et.al., 1997) have highlighted the context in which agreements emerge and how the divergent interests of the actors are expressed in the substance of the provisions which are negotiated. As a rule an EWC agreement also marks the first step towards transnational interaction between corporate managements, employee representatives, national employee representatives, and trade unions. It represents a preliminary 'constitution' which permits of very different developments, and which often requires revision after only a short period. The development of the interactions between and within these groups of actors is often highly dynamic in character (Lecher et.al., 1999; Platzer and Weiner, 1998 and Chapter 2 above).

As far as their function is concerned, EWCs initially reveal a fairly homogeneous picture. In 99 per cent of all agreements looked at by Marginson et.al., the reference to the forum's function corresponded with that of the section on information and consultation in the Directive. In most cases, the function of consultation – in accordance with the Directive – was denoted as dialogue or as an exchange of views. Only 7 per cent of agreements moved on to define consultation as a formal procedure through which opinions can be expressed. Moreover, in 6 per cent of agreements, the EWC was assigned a 'proactive' role.[6] This category embraced the 4 per cent of agreements in which EWCs have the right to make recommendations and put forward their own proposals, and the 2 per cent of agreements which allow for negotiations between management and employee representatives on specified issues. Agreements in undertakings headquartered in France and Belgium were more likely to provide for an active role for EWCs than those in Italy and Spain. The probability was lower for companies headquartered outside Europe (Marginson et.al. p. 25). Looking at the wording of agreements, the study concluded, 'that the scope of the involvement accorded to employee representatives on EWCs remains within the boundaries specified by the Directive: EWCs are about information and consultation' (ibid. p. 26).

The degree of divergence between agreements was found to be greater on the question of which issues can be dealt with by EWCs. All but six agreements specified issues considered to fall within the competence of EWCs. In descending order of frequency from almost 100 per cent to a little over 10 per cent these included: the economic and financial state of the company, employment and social issues, production and sales, investment, new working methods and technologies, structure and organisation, transfers of production, mergers, acquisitions, cutbacks, closures and redundancies, health and safety, environment, training, and equal opportunities. This is not an exhaustive list, as the other issues cited by Marginson et. al. indicate (Marginson et. al., 1998, p. 32). However, although the list of agreed issues reflects the Directive's subsidiary requirements, it is noticeable that restructuring as such – that is, transfers, cutbacks, closures and collective redundancies – was only mentioned in around half the agreements. In addition, it cannot be inferred from the issues specifically cited that other issues might not be important in exchanges between management and employee representatives: either they may not need to be expressly addressed because they, as Marginson et.al. observe, are a 'normal ingredient' of such exchanges or they might be dealt with within the framework of information and consultation at national level. Moreover, a tightly-specified list of issues in an EWC agreement could indicate an absence of national procedures or a lack of trust between the signatories (ibid. p. 27).

The type of EWC specified in the Directive's subsidiary requirements is based on the German model of a body composed solely of employee representatives. However, two-thirds of French agreements prescribed a mixed forum of employee representatives and management. There are marked differences both by country and branch in this respect. The 'German model' was most prevalent in Italy and Spain (71 per cent), as well as in Germany, the Netherlands, Austria and Switzerland (58 per cent). In contrast, the 'French model' was dominant in France and Belgium (97 per cent), in undertakings from the USA (96 per cent) and Japan (93 per cent), in the UK and Irish Republic (89 per cent), as well as in Denmark, Finland, Norway and Sweden (66 per cent) (ibid. p. 20). Whereas joint forums are an established part of the industrial relations landscape in France, the high proportion of such EWCs in Germany, the Netherlands or Austria – in which the norm is employee-only bodies – is noteworthy.

There are three possible explanations for this disparate scene. Firstly, the establishment of a joint body at European level might be seen as forestalling any 'creeping' diminution of the significance of the more influential national body. Secondly, national employee representatives at corporate HQ might see their strong position vis-à-vis management as being better safeguarded through a weaker European body (ibid. p. 20). And thirdly, it may be that a degree of uncertainty as to the role and function of the EWC on the part of trade unions, customarily directly or indirectly rooted at enterprise or workplace level, has led them to favour a joint body. This view is supported by a comparison of joint and non-joint bodies in branches in which the European and/or national trade unions have played an important role in organising and co-ordinating the conclusion of voluntary agreements. For example, 89 per cent of agreements in the food, drink and tobacco sector were joint, followed by 82 per cent in financial services and 72 per cent in chemicals (ibid., p. 27). A similar degree of uncertainty might be assumed to be at work in the majority of those agreements that were concluded at divisional level rather than for the group as whole: such divisional agreements accounted for 15 per cent of EWCs based on voluntary agreements (ibid., p 29).

There are also differences on the issue of whether the agreement provides for a steering committee to take responsibility for communication and co-ordination between meetings and to serve as a direct link to group management. (The Directive refers to 'select committee': both terms are used in practice. The Directive's subsidiary requirements provide for such a committee where the size of the EWC as a whole requires it.) In fact, fewer than two-thirds of agreements provided for such a committee. And only one third of small EWCs with fewer than 10 members agreed such a committee. In such cases, an individual member often takes on the tasks carried out by a steering committee in larger groups – albeit without any express assignment of powers under an agreement. The question of joint or non-joint composition also cropped up in the case of steering committees; in the agreements studied, 71 per cent of such committees were found to be composed solely of employee representatives (ibid. p. 52).

The agreements exhibited a wide diversity of procedures. For example, on the question of additional or extraordinary meetings of the EWC, 87 per cent of agreements looked at by Marginson et.al. provided for an annual meeting and only 13 per cent for two or more meetings per year. Additional meetings were provided for in some four-fifths of agreements. However, 62 per cent required a joint decision of employee representatives and group management to trigger such a meeting (ibid., p. 59). Preparatory meetings of employee representatives were provided for in 63 per cent of agreements, but preparatory and follow-up meetings in only 22 per cent of cases. In 15 per cent of cases the EWC simply convenes for one joint meeting with management. The political and strategic uncertainties surrounding EWCs are highlighted once again by the fact that substantial number of agreements do not provide for an independent meeting of employee representatives.

Seventy eight per cent of agreements provided for recourse to external experts (ibid., p. 75). However, fewer than a quarter of agreements granted the right for full-time trade union officials to participate in meetings ex officio; a further 14 per cent allowed for them to be invited. Moreover, full-time officials can also attend as guests, observers or experts. Because reimbursement of costs is only granted in the event of invitations extended to experts, this can limit access to specialist expertise. This can be minimised where the EWC has its own budget and hence greater scope to act independently. However, this was provided for in only 10 per cent of agreements (ibid., p. 78).

The low level of formal inclusion of full-time trade union officials contrasts with the central organising and co-ordinating role played by the European industry federations in the establishment of EWCs during the phase of voluntary agreements under Article 13 of the Directive. It was the activity of trade unions which led to three-quarters of all agreements in France and Germany prior to September 1994. In the metalworking and chemical industries the intense engagement of the sectoral trade unions ensured that, once again, almost three-quarters of EWC agreements in the sector were concluded before the adoption of the Directive. The fact that 32 per cent of agreements were signed by the European industry federations suggests a high level of commitment to EWCs on the part of European trade unions (ibid., p. 21). However, this engagement was not always reciprocated by a formally inscribed right to participate in EWC meetings.

In addition to differences by country, branch and company-size, which have led to a broad range of standards in agreements (and which still need more detailed study), the motives and strategic objectives which guided corporate behaviour in the period before September 1996 also need to be considered. For example, whilst most employers were eager for a 'minimal solution', with standards below the minimum requirements of the Directive, others took a more forward-looking stance and built EWCs into broader strategies for information disclosure, reputation management, building a European corporate identity, and transnational human resource management. The predominant aim of employers during the phase of 'enforced voluntarism' was to achieve a customised outcome for their business. European structures for employee information and consultation were to be adapted to 'in house' corporate strategies, which in many cases implied the creation and development of an EWC-related 'bottom up' communication structure within and between decentralised layers of management at national locations and corporate headquarters. The fact that employers' associations found it hard to keep pace with demands for customised solutions from their members also explains why they played a minor – or even no – role in negotiating and implementing EWCs compared with the active service and advisory role played by trade unions, and why their, principally lobbying, role during the adoption of the Directive was confined to the legislative process.

EWCs in the Food, Insurance, and Banking Sectors

The Food Sector

The food sector consists of a large number of sub-sectors (dairy products, confectionery, drinks, sugar, meat etc.), each with a different structure and composition. However, there are some common features. The first is that the food sector in Europe is characterised by overcapacity as a result of market saturation. Expansion is only possible by displacing other suppliers, either by cutting prices and costs or by introducing new products which usually replace existing products; a further option is to expand into markets outside Europe which have not yet been saturated. The second characteristic is that the skill level of employees is fairly high, with a high requirement for employee flexibility. This has led companies to 'treat their employees well'.

The strategy of the major food companies is to concentrate on their core businesses (horizontal and vertical) and globalise. Horizontal diversification is being cut: unprofitable areas of business are being abandoned and product ranges thinned down in favour of a concentrating on businesses which deliver national, regional or market leadership. Companies are busily engaged in buying and selling businesses between themselves, either directly or in a broader circuit. Competitors with strong position in the market are allowed to achieve market leadership in their areas of strength by other companies' selling of their interests in these particular markets. This process began in the late-1980s and reached its zenith in the mid-1990s, since when it has continued at a somewhat lower level. At the same time, companies have sought to reduce their degree of vertical integration ('manufacturing depth') and concentrate on those areas which yield the highest value-added. Parallel to this, large undertakings are building up supply pyramids. This new strategic direction and restructuring are changing the structure of the European food sector: the market power of the larger companies is growing – a fact which is quite consistent with an absolute shrinkage in their size.

The majority of undertakings in the food industry are not international businesses, although many are on the verge of internationalising themselves and adopting a global orientation. Whilst one of the factors driving internationalisation is the pursuit of lower costs, the main objective is market access. The fact that European markets are saturated is leading many formerly national companies to adopt a global strategy without first passing through an intermediate stage of Europeanisation. The preferred areas for investment have been markets offering the best hopes of growth in demand – South America, South East Asia, Australia, and Eastern Europe.

A total of 54 of the some 150-160 undertakings covered by the Directive in the food industry have concluded an Article 13 agreement. In most cases national or European trade unions were involved in the establishment of the EWC. The EWCs in the sector can be divided into three broad groupings, by structure and mode of operation:

- EWCs emerging from the world company council movement which are strongly influenced by trade unions.
- EWCs which are sustained by a strong and professional system of workplace/company employee representation.
- EWCs which have grown out of the tasks of everyday representation in the company, but which are only rarely strategically conceived.

Those EWCs which emerged from the world company council movement, and which bear a strong trade union imprint, normally consist of up to 50 employee representatives. Of these, around a third are full-time trade union representatives who both conduct the ongoing work of the forum and occupy the key posts on the EWCs. Based on its earlier role in the world company council movement, the IUF (International Union of Foodworkers) has assumed a key role in the process. It organises annual meetings, hires space, arranges interpreters and accommodation, and sends agendas to EWC members (only the IUF has the full address list). In addition, a national trade union co-ordinator is appointed in each case. The co-ordinators are responsible for the internal direction of the EWC and are empowered to represent it vis-à-vis corporate management. Steering committees are organised by the trade union and for the most part consist of trade union representatives. The union prepares meetings – for example, selecting the issues for discussion at the annual meeting – and organises a preparatory discussion at which common positions can be agreed. There are few informal contacts between company-level representatives in the intervals between meetings, and the IUF does not seek to foster this. On the contrary, communication is organised such that it always has to pass through the national trade union co-ordinator – a procedure which slows down the flow of information but which ensures that trade union control can be maintained.

The function of the EWC in relation to management embraces both the receipt of information and consultation, together with pushing forward joint initiatives and agreements. Within this process, consultation – understood as a procedure for the active inclusion of the EWC in the decision-making process at the appropriate time – is a relatively recent development. The conduct of management has varied from being welcoming to being initially reserved. Whereas in the first case there were few problems as far as the quality of information was concerned, and joint agreements on industrial relations issues in the group could be concluded fairly swiftly, in the second considerable efforts were needed to raise the standard of information supplied by top management. Agreements were not initially possible.

The pattern of development – from raising new issues up to the adoption of a framework agreement – almost invariably follows a common pattern. An issue amenable to compromise is initially raised by the trade union side. Positions are agreed within the steering committee and via discussions with group management. The steering committee then raises the issue in the form of a working paper within the EWC: where necessary the situation at national and workplace level is assessed by the national co-ordinators. The working paper is discussed in the EWC, modified or supplemented, and subsequently adopted: this then serves as the basis for negotiations with group management. After the conclusion of a framework agreement, implementation at national level is evaluated from time to time.

The union strategy of intense engagement with EWCs allows union concerns to be raised with group managements at European level. However, it is a strategy which is not without its difficulties. On the one hand, capacity limitations mean that it cannot be widely replicated, as evidenced by the fact that the vast majority of EWCs even in the IUF's organising sphere follow another pattern entailing the participation of just one or two full-time officials. On the other hand, the relationship between trade union and workplace EWC representatives has given rise to conflicts as workplace representatives are unwilling to accept a passive role and do not consider that their interests are adequately represented. In part, this is expressed in open criticism of the work of the steering committee. The demand for sectoral committees is also an indicator of the fact that workplace representatives' needs for detailed information is not being satisfactorily met.

Those EWCs underpinned by a strong and professional structure of workplace employee representation have developed along a different course. There are two reasons for this: firstly, the existence of managements who are often hostile to trade unions, who would not have conceded an EWC without the pressure of the Directive and who use every means available to prevent the EWC becoming a trade union institution; and secondly, the presence of confident and professional workplace employee representatives within the EWC, linked to national trade union traditions but capable of acting on their own account. Such a presence allows an effective organisation to be established quickly, and facilitates agreement on common positions and their rapid forwarding to corporate management.

By contrast, EWCs which develop out of current everyday issues can often be traced back to initiatives taken by management. For the most part, they were established shortly before the expiry of the deadline for voluntary agreements and initially served mainly as a means for information disclosure. However, the simplicity and immediacy of the arrangements for both sides make it fairly easy to establish personal relationships and informal contacts. The dynamic seems to be less one of initiation and support from the trade unions, and more one of individual learning on the part of EWC representatives.

The ECF-IUF – the European affiliate of the IUF – has sought to establish a positive reciprocal relationship between trade union and workplace initiatives, and has broad approach to how trade union activity in Europe might be strengthened. Its strategic aim is to achieve the conclusion of collective agreements at European level, both at single or multi-employer level, at sub-sectoral or sectoral level, and at inter-regional level. At company level the ECF-IUF wants to be involved in the establishment of EWCs in order to ensure that they include a trade union dimension from the outset. It also supports collective bargaining by EWCs. Initiatives towards sectoral dialogue are already underway in the hotel and restaurant sub-sector, in the sugar and tobacco industries and in catering. The usual starting points are those issues which concern the industry as a whole. Building on this, attempts are then made to create European trade union structures with the aim of achieving European-level trade union communication and coordination. To some extent, these structures are restricted to regional cross-border arrangements. For example, in the dairy industry efforts are in train to set up a network embracing Belgium, the Netherlands, and the German region of North-Rhine Westphalia. Trade union contacts have also been established in the region embracing Austria, Slovenia, and Italy with the aim of forestalling cross-border relocations of production.

The insurance sector

In 1993 there were some 5,000 insurance companies in the European Union with 30 groups of insurance co-operatives and mutual insurance associations. However, there were only 2,500 wholly independent companies. The branch has some 1.1 million employees, mostly white-collar staff. The companies rely on the services of a further 200,000 insurance intermediaries (brokers and agents), who employ a further 500,000 staff. The number of independent companies and employees has been steadily falling for some time. Although there is not yet a fully-developed single market for insurance in the European Union, a number of Directives have broken up closed national markets for insurance products, creating scope for internationalisation to forge ahead more rapidly. Together with the development of new technologies for information and communication, the opening up of markets as a result of EU Directives has boosted competition and intensified cost pressures, fostering the emergence of universal financial services groups (*bancassurance*) offering an entire range of financial products throughout Europe. The insurance sector has been able to extend its activities by introducing new products at the same time as the opening up of national markets has increased the number of cross-border mergers and acquisitions.

Even were the next few years to be marked by co-operation between banks and insurance companies, rather than mergers and acquisitions, the future for both is seen as lying in establishing internationally-operating *bancassurance* businesses. Insurance companies have competed for some time with the banks for investment business. More recently, partly in response to concerns about the power wielded by German banks over industrial companies via their holding and partly on liquidity grounds, banks have reduced their industrial holdings and entered the insurance business through acquisitions, the establishment of new businesses and co-operation agreements with existing insurance providers. The aim is to capture customers for a range of products.

The trend towards universal financial services groups is most pronounced in France. Such groups need far fewer staff for distribution and investment administration than usual financial services businesses. If the productivity achieved by French *bancassurance* groups were applied to the insurance sector as a whole, some 345,000 posts out of the 900,000 in the industry could be at risk. For Germany, the ratio is 105,000 out of 250,000, in the UK 90,000 out of 220,000, in Switzerland 9,000 out of 36,000, and in Sweden 6,000 out of 19,000. The figures are particularly striking in the case of Austria where 21,000 out of a total of 32,000 could lose their jobs were French productivity levels to be achieved.

Cuts in employee numbers have been underway since the mid-1990s, with every expectation that this process will accelerate in the future. The large administrative apparatuses maintained by insurance companies offer a ripe target for rationalisation. As with banking, insurance is marked by a stark segmentation of its internal labour market between field sales forces and in-house employees. Field sales employees work increasingly autonomously using laptop computers with direct access to company mainframes, in contrast to the previous mode of operation which required close co-operation with in-house staff. Cuts in in-house staff are having an impact on the shape of vocational training, with a much greater focus on field sales and customer liaison skills. This change is fostering a change in culture in which the traditional insurance staff employee is being transformed into a salesperson.

Twenty-nine insurance companies fall under the EWC Directive. In contrast to banking, almost all have concluded voluntary agreements and all these were concluded between 1994 and 1996 during the phase of 'enforced voluntarism', often shortly before the deadline. The first agreement was struck at AGF in 1994. In some companies, such as Allianz, arrangements were already in place for employee information at group level prior to the EWC agreement – in a number of cases dating back to the 1980s. However, the real impetus came from the opportunities for employee contact afforded by EU budget line 4004. This allowed a number of meetings to be held to which employee and trade union representatives were invited. The unions CFDT (France), DAG (Germany), SETCa (Belgium) and MSF (UK) were particularly active. As a consequence, a large number of voluntary agreements were concluded. FIET, the international trade secretariat for workers in finance and commerce, participated in most of the negotiations, and encouraged managements to conclude voluntary agreements on cost grounds.

As far as managements were concerned, EWCs were seen as information committees. Although some agreements contained provisions with potential scope for negotiating on issues at European level, with few exceptions managements are not generally prepared to accept this. Employee representatives also need to build a larger reservoir of mutual trust before being able to engage in negotiations. Possible negotiating issues have included general employment matters, training, reward systems and salary levels.

None the less, employee representatives have high expectations of what might be achieved at European level. German employee representatives would like to develop forms of co-determination in line with their domestic practice. At the same time, it is recognised that EWCs need to focus on strategic corporate issues or, in a slightly weakened form, on the personnel and social ramifications of corporate policy. However, this strategic perspective is absent when the European context for national action is accorded only minor significance, although there is an awareness that the significance of EWCs will grow – not least because of the impact of the euro, which will foster the emergence of a European labour market at corporate level.

German employee representatives must mainly draw on their own resources on EWC issues. They receive information neither from FIET nor from their own union on operational issues. Despite the fact that corporate structures have long been internationalised, the trade unions have remained strongly focused on the national level – with the notable exceptions of DAG and SETCa. Steps to tackle this in ways which would improve union support for EWCs are taking place only gradually. Moreover, the trade unions also seem to be overstretched by the need to develop fresh strategic approaches.

The trade unions in the financial services sphere were not pioneers in establishing EWCs. Some national unions, such as the German HBV, have not accorded a high priority to EWCs and have retained a predominantly national approach. For its part, FIET has a perspective which extends beyond Europe and because of the global orientation of banking and insurance would like to develop EWCs into 'World Councils'. This is of particular relevance to UK-based financial institutions, and increasingly so for undertakings from Continental Europe. FIET's approach is intended to counter the problems that will arise for EWCs where a group's central management is located outside the EU. FIET is, however, aware of the difficulties posed by the creation of World Councils in the light of experience in the 1970s.

Euro-FIET (now part of Union Network International-Europa) has not had its own independent organisation and its presence in Brussels has been restricted to a small office for conducting lobbying and maintaining contacts. FIET's political secretaries are responsible for all global regions, including Europe, and FIET has so far resisted calls to invest more in its relations with EU institutions, and create the necessary political and organisational resources to allow this. In company with the international communication workers union and the IUF, FIET has retained its main organisation in Geneva – and hence close to other key international institutions. Setting up EWCs has been at the expense of other world regions because of the need to assign extra resources to Europe. The confederation intended to cut the allocation of officials' time to Europe – which ranged up to 70 per cent in 1996 and 1997 – back down to 25 per cent.

FIET was aware that it could not service all the EWCs in its scope, although most expected this. Moreover, in the main national trade unions do not have an official responsible for EWCs. This raises the risk that EWCs could drift out of reach. At the same time, there is a danger that managements might establish 'union-free' employee relations or even move on to aggressive 'union busting'. FIET also has also had problems with servicing the EWCs on which it is represented, in many cases simply because of sheer pressure of meetings. As a consequence, FIET delegated this task to the largest trade union represented in an undertaking in the parent company's home country. This has caused problems with some managements who are prepared to accept FIET but not representatives from HBV or DAG. In addition, FIET saw itself as stretched by the demands placed on it by EWCs which wanted support on planning and strategy. FIET also noted that it lacked the staff and financial resources to offer training and other EWC events, which it viewed as the responsibility of unions at national level.

In FIET's view, experience with EWCs has been mixed. Positively,

- most EWCs have been controlled or dominated by the trade unions, or by trade union organised employee representatives,
- exchanges of information between EWCs were running after two or three meetings,
- there was growing intensity of contact between EWCs and trade unions,
- EWCs had opened up a new field for recruitment for the trade unions,
- there were the first signs of cross-border campaigns, and finally,
- the sharing of information and experience was gradually developing.

These positive developments were set against several negative factors:

- in some cases, EWCs had turned into a tool for group management,
- there was no real process of information exchange and communication between the EWC and management, but rather a simple question and answer ritual,
- employee representatives in many cases did not co-ordinate their activities – sometimes because of trade union competition, sometimes because of a lack of any sanction for poor discipline, or because of a purely national focus and the diversity of interests represented,
- EWCs did not have an agenda or strategy – rendering them susceptible to managements' prescribing its agenda,

- EWCs often got stuck on national, and sometimes peripheral, problems without grasping the strategic nature of the forum,
- EWCs lacked resources (technical, organisational and financial) and support,
- there was inadequate integration with workplace/company industrial relations at national level.

National trade unions in general have difficulties in delegating responsibilities and powers to EWCs. The willingness of trade unions to delegate powers is more developed in the UK and Belgium than in other countries: developments in the Netherlands are also moving in this direction. In France, trade unions are often involved in EWCs because they want to be able to control them. The situation is similar in Germany. In contrast, there is often a poor level of integration between trade unions and EWCs in Portugal and Spain, and to some degree in France. Stagnation in the development of EWCs has also created problems in Italy, although the overall number of multinational companies headquartered there is small.

The banking sector

Banking was marked by a major transformation in the late-1980s. Up until then, expansion in business volumes had been matched by a growth in employment, although the operational side of the business had experienced steady rationalisation. Job cuts only began in 1987/88. Since then, employment and turnover have been largely decoupled in the pursuit of 'lean banking'. The restructuring of the banking sector is primarily aimed at operational and organisational aspects, with product innovation occupying second place. In general, the euro is expected to intensify competition between banks in Europe – with severe rationalisation expected in Germany, for example. Global financial deregulation together with broader economic globalisation is not only putting banks under enormous competitive pressure, but also sharpening the competition between banking and insurance.

The origins of restructuring in banking can be found in the intensification of competition (for example, via benchmarking), technical development, and a greater – and increasingly exclusive – pursuit of shareholder value, with target returns on capital of 15-20 per cent. Greater competition has been driving the recent drive for banking mergers, with both 'global' as well as 'European' forces at work. Whilst globally the critical factors are corporate size and being represented in important markets, in Europe the main role has been played by the arrival of the Single Market and EMU. Overall, there is a trend towards fewer but larger businesses. Trade unions are not opposed to mergers as long as they lead to an extension in business opportunities. However, mergers also accelerate a change in management style towards a more US American approach. In addition to mergers, technical rationalisation has also led to job losses in banking and insurance. The reduction – at some 25 per cent – is a phenomenon seen all over the world.

Restructuring is also leading to a greater segmentation of internal labour markets, with a separation between operations and sales. Backoffice functions are being increasingly automated, with poorer and more insecure prospects for less-skilled staff. Moreover, because operations can be concentrated in one place as a result of technical development, only a rump of activities – possibly 20-30 per cent – remain in the branches. In the medium-term many of these activities will also be amenable to centralisation. Sales and distribution, for which the need to provide customer advice has so far offered what were regarded as fairly secure jobs, has also experienced job cuts since the early-1990s. The main cause has been a reduction in the number of branches as a result of the expansion in the self-service component of bank business. Studies estimate that around 500 branches close every year, a trend likely to continue as nearly all European countries are viewed as being 'overbanked'.

Liberalisation of the market for financial services has also intensified competition between banking and insurance. Despite a debate extending back over a decade and a half, very few true *bancassurance* businesses have yet emerged, with the most advanced developments in Switzerland and Belgium. The question as to whether banking and insurance are partners or competitors has not yet been finally resolved. As noted above, banks have reduced their industrial holdings in recent years, in part as a consequence of the debate on their influence over manufacturing companies and in part to gain liquidity, and have entered the insurance business through acquisitions, setting up new businesses and entering into co-operative networks with the aim of steering customers from one business to another. Whereas bankers have inclined towards using holding companies as vehicles, the insurance sector – which is more active in banking activities such as asset management than the other way around – has favoured strategic alliances. Whether these will be sufficient to withstand the pressure of the market (capturing profits) or are simply a stage prior to full mergers and acquisitions remains to be seen.

Within the EU 45 banks fall under the scope of the EWC Directive. Of these, 26 had concluded voluntary agreements by September 1996, all of which were agreed during the phase of 'enforced voluntarism' and in many cases shortly before deadline. The initiative was taken by the employee side, and EU budget line 4004 facilitated a good deal of movement into the negotiating environment of the banking sector. A large number of meetings were held to which employee and trade union representatives could be invited, with DAG, SETCa and MSF all particularly active. The majority of agreements were concluded in the wake of these meetings. Euro-FIET representatives were actively involved in most of the negotiations. The remaining banks will be subject to the Special Negotiating Body (SNB) procedure.

In all, few problems emerged during negotiations. There were some difficulties in countries with divided trade union movements, including Germany where there was competition between the more active DAG and more passive HBV. In other instances factors specific to individual banks also played a part. However, there are no major differences between the agreements; rather, differences first emerged with the practical operation of EWCs. These included a marked transfer of national structures and procedures to the European level. In most cases, inclusion of Central and East European countries did not cause any problems.

The fact that only 26 agreements could be reached in the banking sector is attributable to three factors.

Firstly, since the level of union organisation is fairly low the trade unions have held back from taking the initiative in some cases to thwart the establishment of 'union free' EWCs.

Secondly, corporate managements have often pursued anti-trade union policies. In such instances, a rapid conclusion of agreements cannot be expected, and negotiations may be broken off.

Thirdly, national works councils have not always viewed EWCs positively. Because of the modest rights of EWCs, the question was raised as to the additional benefits offered by a European forum.

The EWCs in the sample were all negotiated shortly before the expiry of the period for concluding voluntary agreements. No prior need was identified by managements and in the majority of cases employee representatives also saw no reason to take the initiative. The upshot is, on the one hand, little practical experience, and on the other agreements – fostered by the manner of negotiations – which are strongly influenced by the national structures of employee representation. EWCs are dominated by national reference points, although this seems to be subject to processes of erosion.

EWCs are viewed as information bodies by management. Although some agreements would allow for negotiating on issues at European level, managements are not as yet prepared to entertain this in practice. Employee representatives also need to build mutual trust before entering into negotiations. Possible negotiating issues have included employee safeguards during rationalisation, pay systems (such as employee share schemes) and training.

EWCs, Sectoral Social Dialogue and the Europeanisation of Collective Bargaining

The fresh impetus given to the process of European integration by the Single Market project prompted a revitalisation of multi-sectoral social dialogue between UNICE, CEEP and the ETUC in the mid-1980s (Buda, 1998, Platzer 1991, pp. 172ff). This led to a fresh definition of the role of trade unions and employers' associations at European level, and with this of the relationship between statutory and agreed regulation within the employment and social system of the EU, with the social partners given scope to regulate their relationship autonomously. The Maastricht Treaty's Social Agreement, incorporated into the Amsterdam Treaty as the new Social Chapter, enshrined this approach in law and expanded the influence of the social partners on the decision-making process in the sphere of employment and social policy, creating as a consequence the first steps towards corporatist structures at European level (Falkner, 1998). In the wake of this delegation of policy responsibility the social partners can now decide, following consultation by the Commission, whether they want to negotiate on and agree a Commission proposal.[7] At the same time, the Member States refrained from creating a legal framework for collective bargaining at European level. Revitalisation also extended to sectoral social dialogue between trade union and employer industry federations. Here the Commission's initial aim was 'contributing to the creation of a European system of industrial relations and favouring collective bargaining' (European Commission, 1995, p. 28). However, it turned out that 'the original aims were too ambitious and the preconditions for the emergence of a system of collective bargaining at Community level were not yet present' (ibid.). The Commission now promotes – politically and financially – the more informal structure of social dialogue which builds on the greater readiness of trade unions and employer associations to reach joint accords.

European trade unions view social dialogue as a promising initiative which, despite awareness of its political, organisational and institutional shortcomings, is seen as holding out the prospect of building a system of European collective bargaining. Against the background of Economic and Monetary Union, this is also seen as needing to embrace the branch level (Hoffmann, 1996). This orientation towards bargaining on conventional negotiating issues, with its implicit conflicts of interest, complements the option of exercising influence on social and employment policy through social dialogue. The employers' organisations have taken a different stance. They see a potential for 'added value' in the treaty provisions on subsidiarity linked with greater scope for influence on European employment and social policy – with lesser emphasis on the scope for the forms of autonomous regulation which typify classical collective bargaining. Their fallback position is reserved for instances in which an agreement between the social partners can offer a more favourable outcome from the employers' standpoint. As a consequence, UNICE has rejected European-level collective bargaining (Hornung-Draus, 1998).

In 1994, these divergent standpoints led to a breakdown in negotiations between UNICE, CEEP and the ETUC over the establishment of European Works Councils (Danis and Hoffmann, 1995). However, one year later – and under the pressure of high external expectations – the three organisations succeeded in agreeing a framework agreement on parental leave. In contrast, they turned down the option of negotiating on an instrument on reversing the burden of proof on sex discrimination. Negotiations on part-time work, which began in 1996, were concluded one year later with an agreement, which was subsequently adopted by the Council of Ministers. (Some trade union centres – including the DGB – and one sectoral union voted against the agreement without, however, preventing the necessary 2/3 majority being reached on the ETUC's executive committee.)

Leaving aside any judgement as to the substance of these agreements, the facilitation of multi-sectoral dialogue through new or improved procedures within the organisations concerned on issues such as feedback, mandating and decision-making has led to greater 'vertical integration' of these organisations. None the less, the results remain far removed from the cohesion observable at national level. Moreover, as yet, trade unions and employers' associations have not made use of the scope in the EU treaty for initiating negotiations autonomously, acting only after an invitation to consider a proposal by the EU Commission. Potentially conflictual issues remain a problem for social dialogue, in particular as long the employers can refuse to negotiate and the trade unions lack any means to compel them. And even when a threat by the Commission to put a provision before the Council for decision without prior negotiation induces the employers to come to the table, the results still cannot be compared with collectively-agreed provisions at national level (Keller and Sörries, 1998).

Only a small number of agreements have been concluded at sectoral level. Examples include civil aviation, commerce and agriculture. The framework agreement on employment in agriculture was the first voluntary and autonomous agreement at European level to regulate such elements of the employment relationship as maximum working time, daily rest and work breaks and the maximum duration of night shifts. The agreement constitutes the initial point of reference for all collective bargaining in the sector at national level. Social dialogue is also fairly well developed in telecommunications, tobacco and sugar. By contrast, key industries such as metalworking and chemicals, which often exercise a leadership role at national level, have failed to demonstrate anything more than the odd meeting at European level. 'The value-added of dialogue at European level is not always evident to economic actors that wish to profit from competition in the social field' (European Commission, 1998).

Based on the interest of the European trade union industry federations in the development of social dialogue and the promotion of it by the Commission, sectoral dialogue has nevertheless increased. The number of sectors in which dialogue has begun has doubled to 23 since the mid-1980s. In particular, activity has been high in branches undergoing structural transformation. Over the same period, the number of joint positions and recommendations has increased markedly. Although most texts relate to EU initiatives in the economic and social spheres, based on the advisory role of joint bodies within the framework of social dialogue, these institutional limitations have begun to be overcome. For example, since the mid-1990s, traditional employer-union issues such as working conditions and working time have begun to have a higher profile.

With some provisos, this development can also be seen in the food and drink, banking and insurance sectors, in which employer organisations and trade unions meet not in the form of joint committees with Commission participation but rather in informal working parties mostly without Commission involvement, or in discussion groups in non-structured forms of social dialogue. In the food and drink sector, the European Committee of the IUF (ECF-IUF) faces some 70 employer associations, most of which are trade rather than employer bodies. The heterogeneity of the sector has meant that there is no single employer body at European level able to represent all firms in the industry. As a consequence, social dialogue has been concentrated in sub-sectors. For example, the European agricultural employers association and ECF-IUF, which first met to exchange information at the instigation of the Commission in 1968, have concluded an agreement on a joint working arrangements in which both sides have reiterated their commitment to improve mutual dialogue. This has included a project to reduce the number of accidents in the sugar industry. In 1997, there was an agreement in the tobacco industry between the ECF-IUF and GITES (the trade association for the tobacco industry) which set out the aims and structures of social dialogue. The two sides intend to exchange information and co-ordinate efforts on social matters within the industry. ECF-IUF and HOTREC, the employers' association in the hotel and catering industry for the EU and EEA, have also maintained contacts and issued joint statements since 1984 (for details, see Sörries, 1998, pp. 161ff). These have dealt with value-added tax and its impact on companies and on employment (1994 and 1997), employment retention and creation in tourism in rural areas (1995) and working time flexibility, part-time work, and job creation (1995). The ECF-IUF also maintains informal co-operation with the employers in the dairying and brewing industries. By contrast, contacts have not got off the ground in the coffee, baking and confectionery, slaughterhouse and meat sectors.

In banking, social dialogue was institutionalised via an informal working group in 1990. Ad hoc meetings had taken place since 1978. The working group consisted of 15 participants from trade unions represented in Euro-FIET and the same number from employers' associations affiliated to FB-UE (Federation of Banks in the European Union) and EACB (European Association of Co-operative Banks). As yet activities have focused on seminars and studies. For example, a seminar was held on employment in banking (1989) with further seminars on personnel planning and vocational training (1990) and on the development of employment in the sector (1995). A study was also commissioned on the social consequences of mergers in the banking sector. As yet no joint opinion has been issued. However, both the trade union and employer sides are now more interested in being involved in the development of the EU's social policy than previously. The reluctance of the employers to formulate joint opinions and recommendations means, however, that negotiations on framework agreements in the banking sector are still some way off.

Social dialogue in insurance has involved the establishment of an informal dialogue group, in 1987, by European regional organisations of the International Federation of White-Collar Staffs, Euro-FIET, and the European employers' association, CEA (European Insurance Committee) and ACME (European Mutual and Co-operative Insurance Association) and BIPAR (International Federation of Insurance Intermediaries). The group consists of 15 trade unions and 15 employer representatives. Working groups to monitor ongoing studies have existed since 1995. The first joint opinion was issued in 1996. This dealt with the development of social dialogue by the Commission with a focus on the issues of employment and training.

The main outcome of more than a decade of activity by the dialogue group has been a series of studies. One study and a seminar dealt with the consequences of the introduction of IT and the completion of the Single Market (19898/89); a further study looked at quantitative and qualitative aspects of employment in the insurance sector (1995/6), and another considered the feasibility of establishing an observatory on employment in the insurance sector (1995/6). FIET and the employer' organisations agreed to focus on social dialogue in employment and vocational training. The aim was to be able to anticipate the expected changes in the insurance sector in order to ensure that developments could be steered in a way which would take account of the social concerns of employees. The planned observatory is intended to provide the national and transnational participants in the social dialogue with the necessary data. However, the employers refused to allow the observatory to investigate the qualitative and quantitative aspects of employment.

As far as the European Commission is concerned, as 'process manager', social dialogue in the insurance sector suffers from a contradiction (European Commission, 1995). Although trade unions and employers' organisations want to strengthen their influence at the European level and bring this to bear on issues of concern to them, the employers view social dialogue merely as a means for exchanging information and non-binding consultation on social policy issues. They have rejected issuing joint opinions on specific issues – let alone negotiating on them. Euro-FIET wanted a more constructive approach to dialogue from the employers and pressed the Commission to promote social dialogue more forcefully. FIET noted that some employer associations have only participated in social dialogue in order to gain recognition as 'social partners' as European level, and through this be informed and consulted on policy issues themselves. As a consequence, FIET called on the Commission to provide financial support for social dialogue only where there is active participation from the organisations involved. It expected that – without underestimating the resistance from employers' associations – these political and financial incentives could lead to greater readiness from the employers to negotiate at European level.

The development of social dialogue in the food and drink, banking and industries has generally met with a cool reception from the employers. The initiative to begin and institutionalise talks, together with setting the overall agenda, has come from the trade unions. Employer participation in joint committees has secured them the status of social partners at European level, affording scope for them to be incorporated into the Commission's policy-making process on a routine basis. This also raises the prospect of participation in the EU's research and promotion programmes. In addition to these objectives, which are focused on the EU's political institutions, there is a gradual but growing preparedness to extend information and an exchange of views with the trade unions in the direction of joint opinions, recommendations and agreements. Neither the current horizontal nor vertical intensification of social dialogue suggests that a fundamental transformation is imminent. However, at sectoral level the emergence of some degree of willingness on the employers' part to consider employment and social issues in the form of joint initiatives as a means of giving substance to the fact of their mutual recognition as social partners has meant that social dialogue at this level is slowly moving towards the prospect of framework accords: these could, in turn, constitute a framework for national-level collective bargaining.

Awareness of the problems of social dialogue, together with the creation of Economic and Monetary Union, has led the trade unions – for example, in the engineering industry at national level with the involvement of the European Metalworkers Federation (EMF) – to adopt a new approach to how European collective bargaining should be configured (Schulten, 1998). Whilst the new conditions of exchange and competition within the EU have raised the mutual impact of national collective bargaining, the lack of a political mechanism within EMU could generate more intense competition between national systems. The development of 'competitive corporatism' (Rhodes, 1997), which subordinates collective bargaining to the dictates of maintaining national competitiveness, might, on this analysis, culminate in a 'race to the bottom', especially as collective bargaining will be a central tool of economic adjustment in the absence of exchange rate variations between EMU countries. Within EMU any lowering of national competitiveness would have to be offset by wage concessions (Busch, 1994). On the other hand, the trade unions expect that EMU will render regime competition and the competitive economic environment 'more transparent and create new possibilities for a re-orientation of collective bargaining strategies at European-level' (Schulten, 1998).

Building on the experience gleaned from the activities of the EMF's collective bargaining committee, which was established in the early 1970s, the trade unions affiliated to the EMF have now set out to prevent 'wage dumping' through greater co-ordination of collective bargaining and the establishment of guidelines for collective bargaining, based on a formula rooted in inflation and productivity growth. The first step involves the creation of an information system on collective bargaining developments at national level, exchange of union negotiators, the involvement of foreign collective bargaining specialists in national bargaining rounds, synchronisation of bargaining, European campaigns and the development of cross-border forms of action and protest. This horizontal intensification of cross-border trade union communication and co-operation is intended to underpin the commitments expressed in EMF resolutions on collective bargaining. Vertical trade union relationships have also been restructured such that the EMF now has a mandate to elaborate proposals for minimum European norms on working conditions. One initial result of this is the establishment of a maximum annual working time of 1,750 hours.

What remains unresolved is whether this initiative constitutes a new path in the Europeanisation of industrial relations and collective bargaining – one which entails increasing independence from transnational or supra-national structures (Keller and Sörries, 1998). Unanswered in this context is the question as to the desirability and feasibility of the European industry federations' possible role in the co-ordination of national collective bargaining and the allocation of trade union functions and resources to different levels. Developing an international strategy without the systematic inclusion of existing approaches to the supra-national dimension of industrial relations would ultimately weaken the latter, both institutionally and politically, as the European level depends on the active support of the national level – a support which could scarcely be guaranteed if the two were in competition. Greater autonomy for European industrial relations could not really be attained as it would become more reliant, both politically and financially, on the Commission (Martin, 1996). Finally, it would also undermine trade union calls for a legally and politically supported extension of trade union capacity and capabilities at European level.

Notes

1   The option of setting up a decentralised procedure for information and consultation provided for in the Directive had barely been made use of up until the deadline for the conclusion of voluntary agreements. However, the hostility to EWCs by some managements is likely to mean that this procedure could be used more in the future.

2   The European Union together with Iceland, Norway and Liechtenstein.

3   Transposition in the UK took place in December 1999, following the extension of the Directive to the UK in December 1997 – with a two year period of transition during which companies not previously covered by the Directive by virtue of the exclusion of their British workforces could conclude 'voluntary' agreements on information and consultation.

4   European Commission, 'Draft Directive on national-level information and consultation of workers' (COM98/612).

5   The numbers used in the literature vary according to the basis used. The data here relate to the texts of agreements in the survey conducted by the Dublin Foundation (N = 386) and the figures from the ETUI on the overall numbers of undertakings within the scope of the Directive (N = 1, 114). These numbers are used here, unless otherwise indicated. As noted in Chapter 1, there are higher estimates of both the numbers of agreements and of the number of companies within the Directive's scope.

6   However, these agreements were concluded before the adoption of the Directive in September 1994. This strengthens the assumption that in order to maximise the number of

voluntary agreements (in the period 1994-1996) the trade unions accepted weaker provisions on EWC functions.

7   In the event of an agreement being reached the social partners can choose either on an agreed or statutory procedure for implementation. Either they can implement it autonomously, through their member organisations or in accordance with procedures in Member States, or they can apply for a Decision of the Council of Ministers on a Commission proposal. The first procedure requires member organisations which are able and willing to effect implementation; the second is problematic on grounds of democratic theory as it curtails the participative rights of the European Parliament (see on this and related problems, Sörries, 1998 pp. 21ff.).

3 European Works Councils: Origins, Forms and Dynamics of Development: A Typology

Using typologies to categorise, classify and hence render complex social realities amenable to analysis is a common theoretical procedure. None the less, the heuristic or analytical function and scope of typologies remain controversial – and in particular the degree to which a typology can bridge the gap between description and explanation: that is, whether a typology is always no more than a typology and hence incapable of explaining the categories from which it is composed.

There are two main reasons for attempting a typology in the field of EWCs and the Europeanisation of industrial relations. Firstly, the EWC itself, as an object of research, merits systematisation and generalisation, given its process character and empirical complexity. And secondly, research in the field has now developed sufficiently to allow such an approach. In a more practical vein, establishing a set of distinct EWC types could help trade union efforts to develop a more targeted approach in their support for EWCs and suggest how they might be integrated into other areas of activity. A typology could also offer a starting point for assessing the scope, limits and tasks of EWC networks.

The Diverse Reality of EWCs: Preconditions for and Problems of a Typology

The need for and conceptual and analytical problems entailed by a typology of EWCs are the product of i) the external context and ii) internal developmental preconditions of EWCs.

The process through which EWCs became established and developed, beginning with the voluntary agreements of the French 'pioneer projects' in the mid-1980s, now extends back over a decade. By the end of 1996, some 460 EWCs had been set up, of which at least 90 per cent had been established between September 1994 and 1996 under the procedures for voluntary agreements under Article 13 of the EWC Directive. Between 1996 and mid-2000, a further 170 were established under Article 6 of the Directive (which requires the establishment of a Special Negotiating Body following a request by employees). Negotiations were reported in train in a further 150 cases.[1]

As a consequence, EWCs are still both relatively 'young' and – in terms of their transnational structure and objectives – novel forums for information and consultation at European level. EWCs represent an experimental field for transnational workplace industrial relations and their activities are often still characterised by the search for appropriate practice and strategic focus. Their internal structure, cohesiveness, strategic direction and capacity for information, consultation or negotiation all vary considerably.

The diversity of EWCs and the lack of uniformity in their operation is due, in the first instance, to the specific characteristics of the companies in which they are established and the circumstances under which they were constituted. But it is also attributable to the particular political and legal approach adopted in the Directive which, in its interplay between freedom of contract and mandatory regulation, demonstrated a 'successful, but also (and possibly on account of it) compromise-based path for the creation and application of law' (Höland, 1998, p. 67).

In contrast to earlier attempts to develop a European-level legal instrument for employee participation and co-determination – such as the Vredeling Directive – which envisaged standardising practice, the EWC Directive is rooted in subsidiarity, the provision of options, voluntarism and the specification of procedures rather than outcomes.

However this lack of specification does not mean that the instrument is necessarily weaker. Rather, its effectiveness is achieved in a different way – through practical operation. And since this practice mainly rests on enterprise-level agreements, the current diversity observable in the theory and practice of employee involvement and participation in the Member States is likely to continue to grow at this level, at least for a transitional period (cf. Höland, ibid).

Are all EWCs therefore different? Or is it possible to identify structural patterns in the development and form of EWCs which allow – and indeed require – the establishment of a typology?

Quantitative Research into EWCs – Case-studies as the Basis for a Typology

'Quantitative' studies of existing EWC agreements, focusing on structural indicators, constitute an essential and indispensable basis for more 'qualitative' interpretation and analysis. Several such studies already exist. Marginson et.al. (1998) embraces 386 EWCs and provides information on a range of indicators (country of origin, coverage, and distribution by sector) as well as basic structural features related to the composition of EWCs – for example, that a third of EWCs are employee-only bodies, with management represented on two-thirds. Finally, the study details the preconditions for the practical operation of EWCs as specified in their agreements (such as resources, frequency of meetings, agenda setting, and participation of external advisers).

However, understanding the real import of agreements – that is, the actual development, formation, potential, scope, and focus of EWCs – requires comparative case-studies based on qualitative research.

The present study, with its 15 case-studies from banking, insurance and the food industry, and the previous study by the authors (Lecher, Nagel and Platzer et.al. 1999), which analysed eight companies in the chemical and metalworking branches, set out to match this requirement. Given an empirical foundation of 23 case-studies in five branches, it would now seem possible to envisage attempting a 'provisional comparative, analytical conclusion at a meso-theoretical level' (Höland, 1997). Elaborating a typology of EWCs is intended to offer a taxonomic, classificatory and analytical means of approaching this goal.

An EWC Typology: Assumptions and First Steps

In the first instance, developing a typology of EWCs is an inductive procedure inasmuch as qualitative and quantitative data is used to ascertain whether the structural and process features of EWCs have clustered sufficiently to make them amenable to classification. In essence, however, the creation of a typology is primarily a deductive exercise. That is, the categories, yardsticks and dimensions for identifying distinct types are derived and developed from a pre-existing 'theoretical stock' and from analytical approaches regarded as being of *a priori* relevance to the object of study.

Fundamental to this is an analytical understanding of the constitution of EWCs that conceptualises the overall process of their establishment and development as a product of a dynamic interaction between 'external' influences (political constellations at national and European level, facilitation and effect of the EWC Directive etc.) and 'internal' conditions (interests of and interaction between the protagonists etc.) (Platzer and Weiner, 1998).

Within this overarching perspective, the creation of a typology is underpinned by an analysis of interests and of actors. The corresponding premises and operational criteria are set out below.

Finally, the process of specifying categories also embraces considerations on the multi-level character of European frameworks for decision-making and policy development. Based on the central question as to the status and prospects of EWCs within the overall framework of changing national – and emerging transnational – industrial relations in Europe, EWCs are not solely considered in terms of the customary perspectives of comparative industrial relations research, such as the convergence and divergence of national industrial relations systems in general and the workplace level in particular, or the perspectives for 'Europeanisation' derived from this. Rather, the typology begins with the central issue as to what functions EWCs can fulfil as cross-border institutions, and what status and scope as an actor they have and can acquire.

This allows further consideration of the current and prospective role of EWCs in a multi-level structure of industrial relations in Europe – as now complemented by a transnational enterprise level. Only once this step is complete is it possible to turn to the wider questions of the networking of EWCs, what role they might have in developing sectoral-level industrial relations or the transnational co-ordination of collective bargaining, and finally the possibilities for a 'European multi-tier system of industrial relations' (Platzer, 1998a).

An EWC Typology: Dimensions, Indicators, Categories

Four Fields of Interaction

Given the appropriate internal and external conditions, an EWC passes through an internal process of constitution in which it can progressively attain the status of an industrial relations actor. Although constituted via the actions of its members, it is not autonomous. The pace, direction and course of this process are also shaped by the related actions of others, in a process in which activity both determines and is determined by the EWC's structure. An EWC is constituted via a process of interaction and obtains its specific shape from this.

Four fields of interaction can be distinguished.

1)   EWCs and management

2)   Internal EWC

3)   EWCs and national employee representation

4)   EWCs and trade unions.[2]

Field of Interaction I: EWCs and Management

Two dimensions are critical in this field: to what extent does management grant the EWC, voluntarily or as a concession, firstly scope to operate and secondly scope to participate? The degree of operational scope can be read off from the resources (time, money, facilities) which group management makes available to the EWC together with the degree to which the EWC is able to shape joint meetings with group management. Finally, especially crucial for an EWC's quality as a social actor is its scope for participation along the three tracks of information, consultation and negotiation.

Based on the current state of the practical operation of EWCs, we propose three categories for consideration:

1)   'Deficient' information exchange

Group management's provision of information is poor – either through its being too scanty, not supplied at the appropriate time, not supplied regularly, only disclosed orally, or only supplied incompletely or not at all on important issues. At the same time, the EWC might be a mere passive recipient and refrain from demanding improved performance from group management.

2)   'Satisfactory' information exchange

Group management does not resist meeting its obligations in the information field. For its part, the EWC is active, and successful in obtaining information from management, and gradually succeeds in raising the quality of the information it receives. It is provided with information between regular – usually annual – plenary meetings. Oral and written questions are answered satisfactorily

3)   'Information plus'

The EWC has scope for participation vis-à-vis group management beyond the receipt of information (participation in management's information process). This can range from projects jointly initiated and implemented by management and EWCs,[3] inclusion in the decision-making process in the form of a formalised consultation procedure, up to negotiations and agreements with group management. (We distinguish here between consultation and a formalised consultative procedure. The EWC Directive defines 'consultation' as an 'exchange of views and establishment of dialogue between employees' representatives and central management or any other appropriate level of management'. What is not established is at what stage of the decision-making process consultation must take place, nor even whether it must take place before a decision is taken. It is also not clear whether consultation can postpone a decision. Only when these issues have been resolved can one speak of a formalised consultative procedure.)

Field of Interaction I: EWCs and Management	
Dimensions	Indicators
Scope for activity	
Money	Own budget and financing
Time	Pre- and post-meetings, independent EWC and steering committee meetings, scope for EWC work
Infrastructure	Office, administrative staff, communication
Control of meetings	Setting the agenda, chairing, deciding on time and place of meetings
Participation	
Information	Degree of detail, timeliness, whether provided in writing, continuity, type and relevance of issues
Consultation	Scope, type and relevance of issues
Negotiation	Scope, type and relevance of issues

Field of Interaction II: Internal EWC

The key dimensions of this field of interaction are the EWC's internal capacity and cohesion. Internal capacity presupposes internal structures, procedures and individuals as well as a definition of fields of activity. The pattern of relationships (social configuration) of the forum is marked to varying degrees by relationships of super- and subordination (such as between parent company and subsidiary) and lines of cleavage along issues such as language or business units/divisions. The following structures can be distinguished:

1) hegemonial structures (= accepted dominance)

2) open conflict (= contested dominance)

3) concealed conflict (= dominance is reluctantly tolerated)

4) simple or complex divisions in the structure, and

5) equality (cohesion).

Since most EWCs are still in the early stages of their constitution, relationships are still unstable. As a consequence, it is not usually possible to allocate an EWC to one of the above categories but, at best, to point to possible trends.

Field of Interaction II: Internal EWC	
Dimension	Indicators
Capacity	
Structures	Operating structure, communication structure, informal structures
Procedures	For information exchange, for agreeing and co-ordinating interests
Actors	Engagement, numbers
Fields of activity	Type and relevance
Structure	
Parent-company dominance	Composition
Trade union dominance	Composition, leadership and decision-making structures, division of function between trade union and workplace representatives
Language group	Factionalism, inclusion/exclusion
Interest groups	For example, by business divisions
Inter trade union competition	Ideological differences, impacts on EWCs

Field of Interaction III: EWCs and National Employee Representation

This field embraces the interface between the European and national level of employee representation. The decisive factor is whether and to what extent there is a mutual exchange of resources between the two levels.[4] Information is important, but is only one of the resources which each level can put at the disposal of the other. Others include infrastructural services, time, capacity, and power – both to take action and to prevail vis-à-vis management.

Field of Interaction III: EWCs and National Employee Representation	
Dimension	Indicators
Resource transfer from national to European level	
Infrastructure	Means of communication, equipment and staffing
Time and capacity	Time off
Capabilities	National strengths, contacts with corporate management
Information	Local information, information via national representative structure
Resource transfer from European to national level	
Infrastructure	Means of communication, bodies
Time and capacity	EWC representatives as supportive force (problem and conflict resolution)
Capabilities	EWC representatives as supportive force (problem and conflict resolution)
Information	Strategic information, information from corporate management, cross-checking with other information
European 'value added'	Success in consultation and negotiation, project results

Field of Interaction IV: EWCs and Trade Unions

The relationship between EWCs and trade unions cannot be judged solely by the degree to which trade unions are formally included in EWCs or in the process of information exchange, or by the degree to which trade unions directly support EWCs, either with expertise or through offering a strategic focus. One equally important criterion is whether and to what degree EWCs and trade unions, irrespective of whether they act independently of each other, co-ordinate their actions and their interests and lend each other indirect support – in particular, whether and to what extent, EWCs pursue policies which relate to trade union priorities and to which trade unions use EWCs to foster the transnationalisation of trade union work.

Field of Interaction IV: EWCs and Trade Unions	
Dimension	Indicators
formal integration	full membership, guest status
specialist and policy support	organisational assistance, training, advice, political focus
resource supplementation and concentration	mutual recognition, agreement on interests and political co-ordination, transfer of knowledge and information

Four Categories of EWC

The raison d'être of EWCs is to take up and deal with those economic and employment-related issues which occur at the corporate level of undertakings or which are of a cross-border nature, as defined in the EWC Directive and its subsidiary requirements. The Directive (and voluntary agreements) assign EWCs the role of 'enterprise-level social dialogue', information and, albeit in a weak form, consultation. However, as empirical studies have shown, the inherent dynamics of EWCs push their development beyond these formal requirements and reveal a potential for, and practice of, both negotiation and more formalised consultation. As a consequence, EWCs can and will acquire a more diverse range of functions and a broader scope.

The study by Marginson et.al. (1998), which examined 386 voluntary EWC agreements, distinguishes 'formal' and 'symbolic' EWCs, on the one hand, and 'active' EWCs on the other. Although agreements are at the heart of the establishment and constitution of EWCs, they often only poorly reflect EWC practice in terms of its dynamics and the non-formal elements and actions which frequently depend on individuals. Our research suggests that the practice of EWCs can diverge markedly from EWC agreements – both lagging and leading in relation to the substance of agreed texts. Qualitative study of EWC practice allows a more complex and accurate picture of EWCs to be established. This, in turn, renders the 'active' EWC amenable to further differentiation.

In our previous study on the establishment of EWCs (Lecher, et.al. 1999), we showed that EWCs are engaged in a dual process of constitution. Based on the fact that EWCs are still at an early stage of institutional development, their practice can be designated as a process of 'search and orientation', with no consolidated structures or defined and demarcated sets of tasks. The typology proposed here therefore begins with how EWCs view themselves, as deducible from their actions and approach, and what can be inferred from what they actually do as opposed to the wishes of individual, or even the majority of, EWC members. The categories begin with the institutional prerequisites and practice of EWCs and also embrace the actions of the partners in interaction where these open, extend or limit areas for future EWC activity.

We identify the following four categories:

1) the symbolic EWC,

2) the service EWC,

3) the project-oriented EWC,

4) the participative EWC.

These categories are rooted in both the origins and evolution of EWCs as well as in an analysis of the interests under consideration and the associated actors. That is, the categories also represent stages in the development 'from a symbolic to a participative EWC'.[5] However, this progression is not inevitable – in two respects. Firstly, an EWC in any category can remain in that category; and secondly, EWCs are not immune from the possibility of regression. In any event, there is no natural course to an EWC's development. Breaks in development are commonplace, especially given the instability of corporate structures. Nor does every EWC have to pass through each stage; for example, an EWC can become participative without first being project-oriented. For some EWCs, service or project orientation could be an entirely appropriate strategy and final destination, whereas for others accepting and exercising influence over an offer of participation from group management might represent the first stage in developing a capacity to implement projects.

The fact that these categories are constructed on the basis of interests and actors, as well as on the process of constitution does, however, introduce some difficulties into how actual cases should be assigned. If an EWC is allocated to a certain category, this can signify two things: either an unstable transitional stage in an earlier state of development or a fairly stabilised EWC which can be allocated relatively unambiguously to a category. In practice there are often hybrids which cannot be unambiguously allocated to any of the categories.

The Symbolic EWC

The symbolic EWC is one which, although formally established, does not truly operate. Activities are confined to – usually annual – meetings with group management. Pre-meetings and follow-up meetings are not used by EWC members to build internal capacity and cohesion. For the most part, EWC members are passive, and allow group management to determine the course of joint meetings. Nor is the EWC in a position or willing, either structurally, organisationally or politically, to obtain and work with information and build up its own resources and capacity to take action above and beyond what exists by virtue of national arrangements. On occasions it might, at best, offer individual EWC members a modest degree of 'European value-added'. Trade unions are only formally included, if at all.

The Symbolic EWC	
EWC and Management Poor information provision – passive EWC	*EWC and National level* No exchange of resources
EWC Internally No capacity No efforts to achieve cohesion	*EWC and Trade Unions* At best formal integration

The Service EWC

The 'service EWC' sees itself as forum for the mutual exchange of information and provision of support between employee representatives. It has a particularly important role to play as an information hub with access to communication channels which allow it to forward and exchange information between meetings. This applies in particular to information from top management which is of interest and relevance to EWC representatives in foreign subsidiaries. EWC members are also active providers of information as well as recipients, both in their interaction with management and between themselves. In addition, they constitute an interface between the European and the national level. The EWC's service functions do not have to be limited to information. It can also intervene locally, either through a select committee or individual leading figures, and offer active support to national or local employees and their representatives.

Service EWCs are constituted internally to enable them to access, process and forward information with a 'European added-value': that is, information which would not have been available nationally or without the existence of a European information and consultation body. However, the EWC's internal structures are not the product of a strategic and systematic construction but tend to develop organically. The EWC functions as a 'service agency' for the national workplace or enterprise employee representation by providing additional information obtained at European- and group-level and via cross-border exchange and the horizontal communication of (national) experiences. The 'European value-added' becomes a 'local value-added' which is of relevance not only but primarily at the level of the group's subsidiaries.

The Service EWC	
EWC and Management Satisfactory information – with active EWC, but no participation above and beyond information	*EWC and National level* Mutual exchange of information
EWC Internally Spontaneously-developed ['organic'] structures and procedures for internal communication which ensure information exchange Sufficiently cohesive to ensure flow of information (mostly hegemonial structure)	*EWC and Trade Unions* Integration of trade unions possible but not necessary

The Project-oriented EWC

The aims and potential of the project-oriented EWC extend beyond those of the 'service EWC', with its primary focus on information. Rather, it is a body which defines and implements projects based on the systematic development of its internal capacities and structures. It defines sets of tasks for itself (projects), which it can implement independently of management. It seeks to consolidate the autonomy of the EWC and build a sustained capacity to engage successfully in negotiations, and other encounters, with management. It aims to open up opportunities for participation over the longer term – scope for which is currently denied it. Its most noteworthy feature is a strategic and systematic approach, expressed in its project-based activities.

Where the development of greater scope for participation is blocked, either by internal obstacles or the restrictive approach taken by group management, a project-oriented EWC will shift to other terrains. In our diagram this means moving from field I to field II, strengthening internal capacity and opening up fields of activity in which co-operation with group management is not necessary.

EWC projects can embrace, for example:

- setting up an independent information system in which information relevant to the EWC can be fed in from individual local operations and subsequently accessed,
- undertaking a systematic comparison of terms and conditions within the group,
- drawing up and agreeing codes of conduct to prevent employee representatives from different locations being played off against each other.

Carrying out projects serves to consolidate and build the transnational body itself, forging trust and an experience of co-operation amongst EWC members as well as creating sustainable structures for practical activity and communication – delivering an 'institutional value-added'. For example, projects could be linked to the establishment of dedicated EWC committees or working parties. Independent projects can also aim at improving services for employee representatives at national or local level, such as providing specific types of information.

The project-oriented EWC creates transnational structures of interaction and produces results which have a 'European value-added' which is primarily experienced at enterprise level nationally. Results can also be used in contexts which go beyond the individual enterprise where they are made available to the trade unions. Finally, projects can demarcate and highlight new issues for negotiation. If the EWC succeeds in inducing group management into such discussions, a focus on projects could easily flow into fuller forms of participation.

The Project-oriented EWC	
EWC and Management Satisfactory information with active EWC participation confined to information	*EWC and National level* Mutual exchange of resources: in particular, transfer of national to European level which strengthens capabilities at European level
EWC Internally Systematic and strategically developed internal structures, procedures and activities which guarantee capacity Sufficiently cohesive to define and implement projects as a body (hegemonial or equal structure)	*EWC and Trade Unions* Integration of trade unions possible but not necessary

The Participative EWC

The participative EWC aims to open up scope for activity and participation beyond the scope of information and consultation, and to move on towards formalised consultative procedures, negotiations and the conclusion of agreements, as well implementing joint projects with management.[6] It sees itself as a body for articulating and representing employee interests, for consultation and for negotiation. It works towards involvement in decision-making procedures and measures which affect employees and for recognition as a negotiating partner. One step towards this for EWCs established prior to or 'in the shadow' of the Directive is to negotiate 'in their own cause' – that is, negotiate with group management to improve the procedures or conditions under which they operate. In this sense, an EWC can only be seen as participative once it demonstrates results. Greater scope for participation may simply be the result of a more expansive position adopted by management. It can rest on the greater capacity of the EWC to assert its interests. And it can also be the expression of a degree of common interest which allows it to work with management within a clearly demarcated terrain.

The doorway to accords and agreements with group management often lies in consensual issues on which joint projects can be initiated or position papers adopted. Negotiations on 'hard' issues, such as pay or working time, entail a complex set of presuppositions related to the internal workings of the EWC, specific constellations of interests (on the part of both EWC and management) and pressures to act which can facilitate processes of exchange. One further possibility for an EWC to raise its scope for involvement consists in making demands for greater inclusion in corporate economic and strategic decision-making processes: that is, a formalised consultative procedure on measures which affect workers in the group as a whole. Both the initial case-studies and the inherent dynamics of EWCs suggest that in practice EWCs tend to go beyond the agreed and statutory basis on which they were established, which sees EWCs as bodies for information and consultation.

The European 'value-added' of a participative EWC is clear and positive from the standpoint of the employees of parent companies and subsidiaries if it deals with issues and resolves problems which lie beyond the reach of national workplace, agreed or statutory arrangements. Such a 'European added-value' might be viewed more ambivalently from the standpoint of national structures of bargaining and representation, especially dual systems, were company-based European negotiations to offer improvements at the price of a decoupling of European from national-level collective bargaining. The relationship could prove detrimental if provisions negotiated under certain enterprise-specific exigencies led to a lowering of national standards. However, the participative EWC could also be a driving force for representation and trade union activity beyond the bounds of the individual enterprise. Negotiations in strategically important companies could have a pilot role for others, creating an impetus to negotiations in the context of sectoral social dialogue.

The degree of Europeanisation of industrial relations at enterprise-level is clearly higher in participative EWCs than in service or project-oriented EWCs. As such, participative EWCs can contribute to the development of a genuinely European level of industrial relations, with consequent feedback effects on national levels as well the promotion of developments at European sectoral level.

The Participative EWC	
EWC and Management Scope for participation beyond information in the form of formalised consultation procedures, negotiations/ agreements and/or bilateral projects	*EWC and National level* Mutual exchange of resources – in particular, transfer of national to European level which strengthens capabilities at European level
EWC Internally Distinct internal structures, procedures and activities which guarantee capacity Sufficiently cohesive to deliver opinions as a body to management and negotiate (hegemonial or equal structure)	*EWC and Trade Unions* Integration of trade unions necessary in their own interest, but not indispensable from standpoint of EWC

European Works Councils in Practice: Case studies

Based on this typology, we now analyse EWC practice in the food, banking and insurance industries, in each case looking at five case-studies. The presentation of the material focuses on the key features of how each was constituted and draws together those aspects which are most typical of the development of each category. Although this approach to the case-studies does have a number of disadvantages – for example, it sacrifices immediacy and means that there is no scope to explore a number of interesting aspects of EWC reality – and although the research material would have allowed for a more detailed and extensive description, for reasons of clarity we decided to give priority to developing the basis for our typology by focusing on what was general and exemplary in the practice and development of the EWCs considered.

EWCs in the Food Industry

There are only broad estimates of how many companies in the food industry are covered by the EWC Directive. Ascertaining a precise number is also complicated by the high levels of restructuring activity in train in the sector. The European trade union industry federation for the industry, ECF-IUF, estimates that some 150-160 companies in its sphere of activity fall under the scope of the Directive.[7] Of these, 54 – a third – have concluded a voluntary agreement under Article 13. To this should be added a much smaller number of Article 6 agreements. Most EWCs were established during the period of 'enforced voluntarism' between 1994 and 1996. Specifically, of the 54 Article 13 agreements, one was agreed in September 1994, two in 1995, 21 between January and August 1996, and a total of 30 in the final month permitted for voluntary agreements in September 1996. In addition, some EWCs have been operating for some time without any formal agreement.

In the main, group managements have not exhibited great enthusiasm for setting up EWCs and have only been willing to do so under the pressure of the Directive. In some cases, although the initiative was taken by group management, this was simply to steal a march on a statutory procedure. Establishing EWCs was the key focus of the ECF-IUF between 1994 and 1996, and the federation succeeded in formally institutionalising its involvement in 32 out of the 54 instances.

The EWC at Oetker

The EWC at the food division of the German conglomerate Oetker is still at a very early stage of development. Aside from the constitutive meeting, held in June 1996, only one ordinary meeting had taken place by 1998 when our research was conducted. As such, at that time the Oetker EWC still largely existed on paper and had brought practically no noteworthy benefits.

The Oetker EWC has functioned essentially as a body for receiving information at the annual meeting, the course of which has been determined by management. The employer side is also dominant in quantitative terms. The EWC itself, with just five members, is a very small body: of these five, two come from the German part of the business, with one member each from France, Austria and Italy. For the employer side, plenary meetings are attended by the group personnel director, the managing director of the food division (both from Germany), and the managing directors of the three foreign subsidiaries. In addition, depending on the issue, other management representatives may attend as experts. At the first meeting, the number of these was so great that 'some EWC representatives had to sit in the second row'. Management presentations took up a large part of the time allocated for the meeting, with little scope for questions and discussion. Moreover, EWC representatives were overwhelmed by information and numbers, and were not adequately prepared for a productive exchange. Of particular note is the fact that management, which had already taken the initiative to set up a European Committee/EWC, also decided to improve the preparedness of EWC members for joint meetings and proposed that pre- and follow-up meetings should be held between annual meetings.

The Oetker EWC is reasonably well favoured as far as establishing operational and communication structures and developing a 'corporate' identity are concerned. The fact that it is not especially large allows informal and personal contacts to be forged between all EWC members. Language problems are of only minor significance. The EWC language is German. The Italian member, the only one who does not speak German, has his own interpreter – his wife, who works in the same plant. There are also opportunities for informal contacts between meetings, although these have no practical impact on how representation actually functions. In particular, EWC members from the foreign subsidiaries seek contact with the German members because the latter have access to top management. They would like to use this channel to obtain information and put forward demands for consideration by group or divisional management. However, the German EWC representatives have only performed this service role to a modest degree.

That the EWC delivers virtually no 'European value-added' and is essentially symbolic in character is not wholly due to the fact that it is still at an early stage of development. It is also a function of the differing interests and patterns of interaction within the forum. It was management who took the initiative to establish the EWC, and German EWC representatives were obliged to climb aboard. However, they were sceptical about the establishment of an EWC as they feared that it would both entail more work and prove detrimental to them, specifically that they would be called on by employee representatives from the foreign subsidiaries to campaign for raising employment conditions up to the, higher, German standard – a fear which was soon seen to be unfounded. Because the company has traditionally pursued a strategy of internationalisation, which did not clash with the interests of the domestic workforce – foreign capacity was only established once German capacity and export possibilities were exhausted – German employee representatives did not see internationalisation as a threat. (Expansion in Eastern Europe could change this approach, however.) As a consequence, they had no particular interest in pushing for their own agenda when the agreement was concluded, nor were they willing to contribute to the development of the body. Conversely, EWC representatives from the group's non-German subsidiaries are too weak to build the EWC themselves. Neither the ECF-IUF nor the German foodworkers' union, NGG, were involved in the establishment of the EWC, nor have they been involved in its ongoing work, and are not therefore in a position to supply any outside impetus.

The EWC at Allied Domecq

So far since its establishment in September 1996, the EWC at the British food company Allied Domecq has viewed itself principally as a body aimed at improving the information available to national employee representatives. This corresponds with the stance adopted by group management, which wants to wield the EWC as a 'soft tool' for the management of the company's decentralised structure, and to build a European corporate culture. As a consequence, group management has been fairly welcoming in its dealings with the EWC and the latter's information requirements. Information has been provided very openly to the EWC at the joint meetings (in theory, annual but in practice more frequent) on the position and prospects of the company, and on measures planned and implemented. In addition, EWC members can communicate between meetings via e-mail or through the EWC chair, the 'co-ordinator', to obtain information from group management. The trust this has engendered also means that the EWC has accepted the boundaries set by management on information disclosure (for example, on pending acquisitions and disposals). EWC members can therefore satisfy their need for information – most of which is concerned with the longer term development of the company which is not regarded as viable in its present form – through direct contact with management. However, they have also already established a dense network of direct links, albeit without the express aim of developing this into an instrument for employee representation. At the centre of this internal communication structure is the Scottish EWC co-ordinator, who is also the main intermediary with group management. The size and composition of the body also favour communication and the development of the EWC more generally. With 13 members, the EWC is still a manageable size and allows personal contacts to be established. The EWC is also fairly homogeneous, with one EWC member for each country. The foreign subsidiaries are in the main relatively small and consist of a single plant. Finally, group management is keen to maintain good relationships: for example, it builds in scope for an informal session during the overall period of the meeting and offers a modicum of entertainment.

The Allied Domecq EWC is an information provider. Its active elements are group management and the EWC co-ordinator. Other EWC members are mostly passive recipients, a role they accept in the confidence that group management and the EWC co-ordinator will pass on information about relevant corporate decisions in good time and without external prompting. Although the EWC sees itself as a trade union-based body, its primary focus is within the company. Full-time trade union officials are drawn on on occasion for advice and support.

The welcoming stance of group management towards the EWC has enabled – and required – it to develop fairly swiftly into a participative body. When the EWC was being constituted, EWC members were drawn into negotiations with group management. In 1995 it took the initiative and invited one representative per country to a preparatory meeting. A representative of ECF-IUF was also allowed to take part in the meeting. It was group management which presented the draft agreement, giving the EWC one-and-half days to prepare proposals for amendments which were then negotiated on. It is also entirely conceivable that group management will bring other proposals to the EWC.

The EWC at Unilever

The EWC at the Anglo-Dutch food manufacturer Unilever was developed with both great speed and determination. In the face of opposition from group management, employee representatives on the EWC succeeded in winning the right to be consulted on the organisation of the annual plenary meeting, and to prevent meetings being instrumentalised by management. Although the joint meeting is chaired by top management, the agenda is drawn up jointly and issues put forward for consideration by the EWC cannot simply be rejected. In addition, the agreement requires that equal time be allotted for presentations and discussion.

The high level of restructuring in train in the group has made this the central issue for joint meetings, together with the corporate strategy that underlies it. The EWC is given general information which goes little beyond what is available in the company's annual report. Group management has notably refused to provide specific information on individual operations, and passes responsibility for this onto national managements.

From the outset, the Unilever EWC has not accorded a central importance to the annual meetings but regards itself as body engaged in continuing activity, and has developed corresponding internal structures.

There is a dual chair, with a German EWC member as chair and a Dutch member as secretary. The chair and secretary meet once a month to discuss and conduct ongoing EWC business. They are the main channels of communication for group management.

In addition, a six-person steering committee, the 'Co-ordinating Committee', was elected: this meets twice a year but can be convened at any time should circumstances require it. The Co-ordinating Committee is a real working body, which 'conducts the everyday business' of the EWC (to quote the EWC Chair). Communication within the Co-ordinating Committee is much more intense than in the EWC, especially as it consists of almost the same people as the negotiating committee which concluded the EWC agreement with management. The language problem is also minimised by the fact that only three language groupings are involved – English, German and Spanish. EWC projects are planned, aired and initiated in the Co-ordinating Committee. The main current project is the development of an EWC information system, the aim of which is to integrate information from above (on group strategy) with information from below (developments at individual locations) in order to be able to anticipate future developments within the group. This would raise the EWC's strategic capacity and give it more confidence in discussions with group management. To this end, a databank project initiated in 1992, but since left dormant, is to be reactivated. A questionnaire was distributed to employee representatives on a wide variety of employment and production issues. The returns were then used to establish the foundation for a database which was kept up to date and extended.

It is also planned to compile a group handbook on policy for dealing with restructuring in the group. This would include agreements already concluded on the issue and would serve as a guide for future restructuring operations. (One model already tested in Germany, for example, involves using some of the funds earmarked for the redundancy scheme to find investors for plants at risk. This has already been used in the Netherlands and might represent an option for employee representatives elsewhere.) The Unilever EWC has also drawn up its own guidelines for dealing with restructuring issues. Amongst other things, EWC members agreed to campaign for an appropriate balance between production, sales and marketing in each country, and in particular that production should not be transferred from smaller countries.

The Co-ordinating Committee functions both as an information as well as a consultative body on specific occasions.[8] At the time our research was conducted, three extraordinary meetings of the Committee had taken place occasioned by disposals of businesses, closures and transfers of production. In all three cases the chair and secretary of the EWC were informed before an official announcement was made. These then called the meetings. The EWC has succeeded in securing – via the Co-ordinating Committee – an active role in the discussion as to how decisions should be implemented. The Committee has also conducted ad hoc negotiations when conflicts have arisen. Group management has been prepared to negotiate as it is itself uncertain how business decisions which it has made ought best to be implemented.

The Unilever EWC has been intensively engaged in scrutinising the group's European policies, and has put forward its own views which have been displayed in all the company's European plants. On the event of Unilever's world conference in early-1999, the EWC held its own press conference in the form of a public EWC meeting, at which it gave its opinion on the company's policy and raised a number of demands for management.

Although the EWC at Unilever is closely associated with the trade unions (individual EWC members have close ties to trade unions and full-time officials attend meetings), the impetus for the development of the EWC comes from workplace employee representatives and is motivated by their desire to have their needs as representatives adequately met.

The Unilever EWC's rapid development is attributable to a number of factors. In the first place, the EWC began to operate not with its formal establishment in September 1996 but in the mid-1980s. At that time, the group works council of the German subsidiary began to campaign for an EWC in order to gain access to information concerning the business at group level which national management had refused to supply. Although group management refused to entertain this prior to the adoption of the EWC Directive in

September 1994, meetings of workplace and trade union representatives began to meet at European level independently of management from the early-1990s – initiated, organised and initially financed by the trade unions. Following the passage of the Directive, group management went on the offensive and pushed for the conclusion of a voluntary agreement. In November 1994, it invited employee representatives to a dialogue conference, at which a negotiating committee was elected. This consisted of one representative each from Denmark (for Northern Europe), Spain (for Southern Europe), Germany, the UK, the Netherlands and Austria; employees from Eastern Europe were not represented. The agreement was strongly contested. The employee side accepted the negotiated compromise under one condition – that the agreement would expire in February 2001 and in the event of a breakdown of new negotiations, the statutory provisions (and indeed that of the Netherlands which provides for trade union involvement) would apply.

Secondly, Unilever does not have a clear national centre in Europe, but rather several national pivots. This means that no one country delegation exercises a 'natural dominance'. As a consequence, employee representatives have been obliged to develop their European work jointly from the outset, to take into account a variety of interests, and to construct the EWC's internal structures accordingly.

Thirdly, this situation only arose because of the presence of committed and skilled employee representatives in each of the national delegations. Although this reflects the generally high standard of senior employee representatives in a big organisation – with all the national subsidiaries of the company broadly equally large in terms of employee numbers – this is only a part of the explanation. The individual skills and personalities of those involved have also played a role, the importance of which should not be minimised.

Fourthly, the restructuring of the group, which is a proceeding at a rapid rate, is anchored in an overall European strategy and, as a consequence, has both a European and a national dimension. The pressure on the EWC to develop a matching response is correspondingly great.

The EWC at Unilever is likely to continue to strive to achieve greater recognition by the company and to extend the scope for its involvement in group-level issues. It has already been able to convince management that its existence offers a number of benefits to the company – as conflict manager, instrument for corporate control and a means of ensuring acceptance for managerial decisions. The EWC Chair, in an interview, alluded to the fact that he thought European-level negotiations were conceivable. With its demand for a European employee share scheme, one test for this hypothesis had already been set in train.

The EWC at Danone

The EWC at the French food concern Danone is one of the EWC pioneers. It developed during a phase in which the group was expanding and became a body with extensive powers and well-honed structures and procedures. However, it must now prove itself during a period of corporate restructuring in Europe. Trade union employee representatives from the company and full-time union officials began to meet at world company council meetings from the early-1980s in a process initiated and financed by the trade unions and without any involvement by group management. By the mid-1980s, the establishment of a European works council had been agreed in correspondence between the IUF and group management. Annual meetings of the EWC have taken place with management since 1986.

Based on the generally favourable attitude of the group chief executive, the EWC and its development were especially important for the trade unions, who were eager to ensure that it could serve as a model for best practice elsewhere. They have continued to be deeply involved. Around two-fifths of the 50-member EWC are full-time trade union officials who, in the main, prepare, manage, organise and direct the meetings. The 30 workplace employee representatives are composed of one member per national subsidiary, including representatives from Central and Eastern Europe. Each national delegation has a co-ordinator – usually a full-time trade union official. These co-ordinators make up the steering committee. The co-ordinator of the French delegation, a full-time official of the CFDT, is the central EWC co-ordinator and first port of call for management.

The Danone EWC has developed an unparalleled culture of negotiation with group management. In 1988 a joint paper was agreed between the IUF, as representative of the EWC, and group management in which each confirmed its preparedness to negotiate on specific issues at European level. The issues cited in this paper became the subject of four agreements concluded between 1989 and 1994.

In 1989 a joint platform was adopted which provided for a strengthening of the information rights of employee representatives at local level. This entailed the compilation of a checklist setting out the minimum amounts of information which had to be given to workforces and their representatives at departmental level, covering business and financial issues, employment, pay and social costs, working hours, health and safety, and training.

At the same time, an action programme to improve equal opportunities between men and women was agreed, with implementation to follow at local level. Existing inequalities found in subsidiaries and at workplace level were to be analysed, and an action programme developed and implemented, with a timetable and monitoring arrangements. The results of the programme were evaluated in the EWC and discussed at the joint meetings.

The programme to promote vocational training was set out in another agreement, concluded in April 1992. This also included an assessment of the current position ('Studies on the Need for Modernisation, Employment and Training'), a listing of the principles to be observed with implementing measures (such as special attention to employees with fewer skills), and an evaluation programme.

Finally, in May 1994, a joint opinion was adopted by the IUF (as representative of the EWC) and group management on the principles for the exercise of trade union rights at local level, which led to a strengthening of trade union rights in the company, in particular in Southern and Eastern Europe.

At the time of our research, negotiations were underway on an agreement to strengthen the rights of trade unions and employee representatives in the event of operational changes which might be detrimental to employment or working conditions. The central points of the agreement, which was on the verge of being concluded, were an obligation on the company or plant management to consult, a commitment to provide training, priority to maintain employment and the possibility of full facility time for trade union or workplace employee representatives in the event of a partial or total closure of a plant. The negotiation and conclusion of framework agreements and their implementation at national and/or workplace level presupposes the development of corresponding structures and procedures; in turn, these drive on further development. The Danone EWC has developed structures and procedures which provide for discussion and agreement on positions within the EWC (including the status of negotiating delegations) and allow for the implementation of agreements.

The conclusion of an agreement usually takes place via the following stages. Initially the IUF secretariat, to which the EWC co-ordinator and IUF official responsible for the group belong, prepares a draft agreement. This is discussed in the steering committee and then submitted in revised form to group management. Management then responds with its own proposals. The steering committee then draws up a response to this. These three texts constitute the basis for the ensuing discussion and arrival at a position at the EWC meeting which precedes the plenary meeting, which also includes a discussion of the drafts. The IUF secretariat then reworks the draft in the light of any criticisms, and enters into discussion with group management.

As a rule, dedicated project groups are set up to implement agreements at national level, sometimes with the participation of both sides. In addition, in some countries the national delegations meet to prepare for and subsequently assess the annual meetings. The impetus for such meetings in part arose from the practical need to implement decisions taken by the EWC.

In order to prepare for agreements, and allow informed discussion with group management, the EWC collects information on a wide range of employment issues in the company, such as training, and health and safety. To this end, it sends detailed questionnaires to local operations, which are analysed by the IUF secretariat prior to meetings.

The EWC at Danone has developed in an exemplary fashion into a participative EWC. A decisive role in this has certainly been the positive attitude to trade unions on the part of group management, which has opened up scope for the unions to build the EWC into an instrument for regulating industrial relations within the group. This also matched management's concern to build stable industrial relations in the company. It uses the EWC as an instrument for personnel management and integration.

The fact that this afforded the trade unions an opportunity to widen the scope of the EWC's participation beyond the provisions of the Directive and towards negotiations, and use the EWC as a model for others, meant they were prepared to invest a good deal of their own resources into developing it and strengthening its structures and procedures. However, the control over the EWC exercised by the trade unions has also served to put a brake on organisation by workplace employee representatives who have remained largely passive and reliant on the country co-ordinators.

Overproduction in the European food sector has confronted the EWC at Danone with considerable corporate restructuring, including plant closures, and management with criticism of its approach to information disclosure. In one instance, although the closure of a site in a foreign subsidiary during the course of the restructuring of a division was centrally decided in France, neither the EWC nor the steering committee was told. The French *comité de group* had been informed about the restructuring and closure, but did not pass this information on to the EWC members affected.

This is indicative of a more fundamental problem. Decisions on restructuring are made at divisional level. However, the decision-making procedures at divisional level are not reflected in the structures of the EWC. As a consequence, the need for EWC representatives from the group's foreign subsidiaries to get hold of information on the status of their operation within the group and the security of their own plants is not being met. However, the EWC's call for the establishment of divisional committees was rejected by group management.

The EWC at Nestlé

The EWC at the Swiss food group Nestlé has met annually with group management since 1990, progressively extending its scope for participation in the face of initial and, with some qualification, continuing opposition from group management.

Developments at Nestlé can be measured by several indicators. Firstly, the quality of information provided at the joint meetings has steadily improved over the years – although it is still regarded as inadequate by EWC members. Although the amount of time allotted to management presentations has been reduced and that intended for questions and discussion extended, management responses are felt to be too tilted towards elaborating on corporate philosophy, with no treatment of concrete restructuring measures.

The EWC also succeeded in negotiating a formal agreement on a consultative procedure in April 1996. This provides for a joint committee to meet in the event of plant closures and transfers of production.[9] Some initial experience has already been gained with the committee. In early 1997 it met to discuss a proposed transfer of production from Italy to France, although a local redundancy agreement had already been concluded in Italy on the matter. In the autumn of 1997 the committee met again to discuss the closure of a Danish ice-cream factory. Although the consultation procedure was properly observed, in that the final decision was not taken until after the meeting, in fact there was no longer any real scope to affect the outcome: the key decision had been taken some months earlier when group management offered the Danish management an investment plan which lacked the resources needed to save the plant. Any real influence on the decision by the EWC would have had to have been exercised at this point. However, holding the committee meeting was not entirely without purpose as it enabled the consultation procedures to be used as an *ad hoc* opportunity to negotiate measures to mitigate the impact of redundancies.

And finally, although group management was for a long time vehemently opposed, there have been some initial steps towards negotiation and the conclusion of European group-level agreements. In 1993, group management adopted a joint paper with the EWC on combating violence and right-wing extremism in the company. This was followed in 1994 by a further joint paper on equal opportunities, which constituted a type of framework agreement for setting and implementing equal opportunities policies at national level.

Although the EWC at Nestlé can look back on a history of steady advancement in its scope for participation in management decisions, established internal arrangements continue to obstruct its further development.

With more than 50 members, the EWC is very large. One third of its members are full-time officials: these carry out the bulk of the work, dominate the body and import their own political and policy differences into the EWC. Moreover, the high turnover of EWC members has impeded continuity. One reason behind this is that the trade unions that delegate individuals to the EWC sometimes replace their entire national contingent. As a result, EWC members have only sporadic contact, and there is no provision for direct contacts within the EWC's formal communication arrangements.

Moreover, full-time union officials occupy the key positions. The EWC chair is a full-time official of the German union NGG, and the EWC co-ordinator is a full-time secretary of the IUF, whose Geneva office is responsible for organisation. The steering committee, which is supposed to prepare the annual meetings and develop the EWC's activities, consists entirely of full-time officials. As yet, it has met only once a year, just prior to the annual EWC meeting and has not committed the required degree of energy to the task. Despite the long-standing existence of the EWC, these structural problems have held back efforts to establish an information system.

The structures and development of the EWC at Nestlé can be explained by its particular origins and history. During the 1970s, full-time union officials and union workplace representatives met once at year at world company council meetings: these ceased in the late-1970s. Around a decade later a European Forum was established on a voluntary and informal basis following an employee initiative, recourse was had to the previous structures, and in particular the IUF re-assumed its key role in the EWC. The EWC was established and developed by trade union officials centrally and systematically 'from above'. Workplace employee representatives had little alternative but to harvest the fruits of the trade unions' work. Not least because of the EWC Directive, which put more emphasis on the role of workplace representatives and reduced dependency on trade union resources, a revision of internal structures and greater reference to local representatives can now be expected.

European Works Councils in the Banking Sector

Some 45 companies in the banking sector fall within the scope of the EWC Directive. Of these, 26 had concluded voluntary agreements by the transposition deadline of September 1996. All the agreements were negotiated during the phase of 'enforced voluntarism' between 1994 and 1996, in many cases shortly before the deadline. The impetus came from employee representatives, with help in getting negotiations under way from financial support under the EC budget line 4004. This allowed a large number of meetings to take place, to which employee and trade union representatives were invited. The CFDT (France), DAG (Germany), SETCa (Belgium) and MSF (UK) were particularly active. Most agreements were concluded in the wake of these meetings. Representatives of Euro-FIET were involved in the bulk of the negotiations. Those companies not covered by voluntary agreements will now have to establish an EWC via the Special Negotiating Body procedure. Given the opposition evident on the part of many bank managements, the number of agreements will probably rise only slowly.

Overall, negotiating voluntary agreements led to few difficulties with group managements. The trade unions had some problems where union movements were politically divided – for example, in Germany where there was some rivalry between the non-DGB DAG white-collar union and HBV, the banking and commerce union affiliated to the DGB. As well as the customary competition between the two organisations, which should be diminished by the creation of a DGB-affiliated 'super' service union ('Ver.di') to which both organisations will belong, the DAG also set about establishing EWCs with greater verve and strategic focus.In other cases, problems specific to individual companies also played a role. However, there are no major divergences between agreements, with most differences emerging only in the course of the practical operation of EWCs (with a marked transfer of national structures and procedures onto the European level). Participation by representatives from Central and Eastern Europe did not usually present any problems.

The fact that only 26 agreements have been concluded in banking is attributable to three factors. Firstly, the level of trade union organisation is comparatively low, with very weak representation in some banks. In such cases, the trade unions have held back from initiating activity to avoid the creation of non-union EWCs. Secondly, group managements have often pursued an anti-trade union policy. And thirdly, workplace employee representatives in countries with developed arrangements for employee representation have not always been receptive to proposals to establish EWCs. Given their modest rights, they asked what extra benefits such a European body would offer.

The EWC at ABN AMRO

The EWC at the Dutch bank ABN AMRO was established during the period in which this research took place, but had not begun operations. As a result, although we were able to document the course of negotiations no information was available about the actual practice of the EWC. The manner in which the EWC was established confirms the feeling that the EWC at ABN AMRO could soon advance beyond the status of a symbolic body to one which will acquire the capacity to negotiate and demonstrate results.

One factor in this is the initiative and engagement demonstrated by the Dutch employee representatives, and also by representatives from some of the bank's individual foreign subsidiaries. The Dutch central works council *(Ondernemingsrad)* took the initiative to negotiate a European forum on a voluntary basis with group management as early as 1992/3. However, management refused to engage in negotiations, with the result that it was only with the transposition of the Directive into Dutch law that the procedure for the establishment of an EWC was officially set in train and negotiations begun with management under Article 6 of the Directive. Employee representatives from the bank's foreign subsidiaries were involved during the preparatory phase, and this informal group formed the core of the Special Negotiating Body (SNB). Trade unions were not involved in the SNB, although the negotiating approach was cleared with Euro-FIET.

The negotiating process itself and the outcome have two notable features. Firstly, the employee side made great efforts to build formalised structures and to draw in employee representatives from the foreign subsidiaries into leadership and operational structures. The agreement provided for a joint select committee (three representatives of group management and five EWC representatives) to meet twice yearly and to serve as an additional source of information. Calls for a technical infrastructure to support this arrangement indicate that the EWC has not allowed itself to be confined to the annual plenary meetings, but wishes to maintain mutual contact. Secondly, the process of negotiation itself indicated that group management was unwilling to depart from its hard line as far as calls for participation by workplace representatives were concerned. Management continues to adhere to the narrow legal requirements and is attempting to keep the EWC's scope for participation to a minimum. From this, it can be assumed that any extension of the scope for employee participation would only follow what could prove to be a vigorous confrontation between the two sides. On the other hand, the EWC – through the SNB, some of whose members will moved onto the steering committee – has already engaged in its first negotiations with group management.

It is still too early for any well-founded judgement as to the direction in which the ABN AMRO EWC will develop. However, should EWC representatives succeed in drawing in the bank's foreign subsidiaries and developing a set of structures, as intended, then it will have a good chance of becoming a project-orientated EWC which, over the long term, will gain in capacity vis-à-vis the company.

The EWC at Bayerische Vereinsbank

The activities of the EWC at the German-headquartered Bayerische Vereinsbank have, as yet, been largely confined to the forum's annual meetings. Including arrival and departure, these last for two days. Representatives of the bank, in rotating composition, join the meetings for around three hours on the second day. Management presentations are intended to convey the bank's culture and strategic objectives to EWC representatives and to foster a sense of common identity. In contrast, the bank has not been exemplary in informing the EWC 'comprehensively and in good time'. EWC members do not receive information prior to meetings and the information which is provided is often very general and given after the event. Although the agreement provides for consultation with the EWC, as yet it has not been practised.

The 16-person EWC does not have a select committee, but simply a praesidium which consists of the EWC chair, their deputy and two 'second deputies', and is more of a leadership than an operational institution. The EWC chair and deputy are both from Germany. The other two positions are held by the Luxembourg and Austrian members. The praesidium does not meet between meetings, nor is there any internal division of labour. All the tasks are undertaken by the EWC chair.

The way in which the EWC has developed so far is mostly attributable to the specific features of the bank's organisation. Bayerische Vereinsbank is not highly internationalised, with fewer than 10 per cent of its employees in foreign subsidiaries. The bank has more than 100 employees only in Luxembourg and Austria. The composition of the EWC reflects this: the German delegation has five members, with one member each from the foreign branches. This has created a particular pattern of interests and behaviour.

German employee representatives had little to gain directly from an establishing an EWC, and the motivation for setting up a voluntary one was due more to other considerations. For example, a voluntary arrangement could be negotiated by the German works councils on its own, without statutory regulation or the need to include employee representatives from the bank's foreign subsidiaries. A statutory EWC would have required it to comply with the formal requirements of the German European Works Councils Law, with the consequence that SNB representatives from foreign branches could have outvoted the German representatives. For the EWC itself, a weighting of votes by employee numbers was agreed.

EWC representatives from the bank's subsidiaries have a particular interest in obtaining information and support via the EWC. Their focus is on the EWC Chair who can obtain and forward information from group management and serve as a channel of communication to management. However, as yet the EWC Chair has only exercised this role to a limited degree, blocking the development of the EWC as a service organisation.

The EWC at Crédit Lyonnais

The EWC at the French bank Crédit Lyonnais has so far only functioned to a modest extent. It is essentially a forum for the receipt of information from management, with its activity confined to the annual plenary sessions and very little contact between meetings. The only exceptions have been occasional questions directed to the EWC secretary, for the most part in the immediate wake of the meetings. Despite its 28 members, there is no steering committee to ensure continuity and communication. The EWC secretary is only elected for one meeting, also militating against continuity.

Group management controls and directs the course of the joint meetings. In the French tradition, it chairs the meetings and compiles the agenda, for which the EWC can propose items eight weeks prior to the session: these are usually accommodated. Issues can also be raised at the last minute under 'Any other business'. Management is responsible for drawing up and distributing the minutes. The meeting itself is attended by group management with the President (Chairman) of the company, the General Director responsible for the subsidiaries, and the European-level personnel manager. Group management provides information on the state of the business and its development. However, concrete information is only provided after measures have already been implemented (such as a disposal). For example, management's response to a question from the EWC about the sale of a Dutch subsidiary was that the decision had not yet been made. Two weeks later EWC members read about it in the newspapers. Although the agreement provides for a right to consultation, this does not go beyond an opportunity to put forward their own proposals – as it were as a supplicant – at the plenary meetings.

The EWC agreement at Crédit Lyonnais was concluded at a very early stage for the sector in 1994. A working party of representatives of the French trade unions FO and CFDT was formed as early as 1989 with the purpose of establishing an EWC. Euro-FIET was involved and negotiations with the company began in 1992. The initiative took place during a period in which the bank was rapidly expanding internationally. It was a trade union project and did not necessarily mirror the interests and activities of employee representatives in the group. Put directly, the trade unions pushed for the establishment of an EWC at Crédit Lyonnais in order to advance the development of EWCs in general, without any particular regard to the circumstances prevailing in the group itself – an approach which has not helped establish a functioning and effective European body.

Workplace employee representatives at the French group did not have any great interest in the establishment of an EWC since they already had access to group management via the French *comité de groupe* and the foreign subsidiaries had only a meagre impact on the domestic activities of the bank. The EWC was seen as vehicle for employee representatives from the group's subsidiaries, and was conceived as such. The low level of interest of French employee representatives in the EWC was translated, given the crisis at the bank, into a national pact with the group's management, whose rationalisation proposals were mainly at the expense of the foreign subsidiaries. This was supported by the French employee representatives – leading to an open breach in the EWC, with the result that the German delegation withdrew and stopped attending annual meetings.

The revision clause in the agreement set for 1998 offered an opportunity for the EWC to negotiate on infrastructural provisions to facilitate ongoing activity and communications. However, it is unlikely – given its internal make-up and the restrictive stance of group management – that the EWC will be able to negotiate successfully. Rather, it faces the prospect of an enduring management blockade.

The EWC at Kredietbank

The EWC at the Belgian bank Kredietbank is the central institution for employee representation at group level. As well as acting as a European body, it also constitutes the point of access for Belgian employee representatives to the group's management. As a consequence, its competence is not limited to transnational issues. The body consists of a national representative body, with 24 Belgian representatives, extended to encompass a few employee representatives from the foreign subsidiaries: two Dutch, one French and one German. The bank's activities are concentrated in Flanders and the Netherlands. Meetings are conducted in Dutch, with interpretation provided for the French and German delegates, leading to some disadvantage vis-à-vis the bulk of those in attendance. However, the concerns of the domestic and foreign subsidiaries are theoretically accorded the same weight.

The EWC sees itself as a service organisation for local employee representation. This has two dimensions. Firstly, it acquires information from group management, raising the level of information available to EWC members. Because group management is relaxed about the EWC, and discloses information quite freely, the amount of effort which the EWC has to expend to

achieve this is not especially high. Secondly, it intervenes to support employee representatives in the event of local problems and conflicts. The scale and
drama of the restructuring of the German subsidiary – with proposed jobs
cuts of some 40 per cent – meant that this took centre-stage in the EWC's
work in 1997. Both the EWC and its steering committee wanted access to
group management to discuss their position and role in the restructuring and
to set out their own views.[10] Although the issue was discussed with the EWC
at group-level, the final decision was considered a matter for national management. Group management gave local management a degree of autonomy
– and hence also freedom to negotiate – which the German managers had disputed. Moreover, the EWC chair and a Belgian member visited the German
subsidiary to assess the situation on the spot and show the EWC's support for
the German works council. The interest showed by the EWC served to
strengthen the hand of the works council in negotiations over a social com-
pensation plan for affected employees. The next issue to confront the EWC
will be the proposed merger between Kredietbank and another Belgian bank.

Although the EWC at Kredietbank is constructed as a 'national forum
plus x', a fact reflected in the quantitative dominance of the Belgian contingent, it aims to deal with problems which affect employee representatives in
the bank's foreign subsidiaries. This may be due to the desire of the Belgian
EWC representatives to respond to the accusations of national dominance
levelled against the initiative. At the same time, group management is interested in using the EWC as an additional information channel and a means of
influencing managements in its national subsidiaries, and therefore supports
the EWC's approach of dealing with national matters at European level.

The EWC would like to advance beyond the service role which it currently exercises and gain a say over group-level decisions, such as the imminent merger or the centralisation of IT – at least as far as dealing with the
effects of these decisions is concerned.[11] The fact that group management is
not opposed to discussions means that the EWC at Kredietbank has scope to
develop into a 'participative' EWC.

The EWC at Deutsche Bank

The EWC at the German bank Deutsche Bank, established in September
1995, was still an at early stage of its development at the time our research
was conducted. Aside from the initial constitutive meeting, only one other
meeting had taken place.

In line with the position taken by UNICE, group management at the bank
initially opposed the establishment of an EWC but changed its stance in ear-

ly-1996. This change of heart can be explained, on the one hand, by its real-isation that a voluntary agreement offered a number of benefits. At the same time, factors specific to the bank also played a role. Group management wanted to introduce personnel management software which would store and process personnel data on a global basis. Under German law, this required the agreement of the works council (in this instance at group level). The group works council (*Konzernbetriebsrat*) made the conclusion of such an agree-ment – with global application – conditional on the establishment of an EWC, in order to allow employee representatives from foreign subsidiaries some scope for consultation on decisions which affected them. Although the agree-ment on personnel software was not an agreement with the EWC in the strict sense, it does suggest that such negotiations might take place in the future. In spring 1996 group management set out its own proposals for an EWC and ne-gotiations with the group works council began.

At the joint meetings, group management has provided information on the issues placed on the jointly agreed agenda. So far, discussions have taken place on the effects of introducing the euro at the bank, the introduction of personnel management software, outsourcing of operations, mergers be-tween the bank's divisions, the establishment of a call centre, and provisions on public holidays. Information was both comprehensive and detailed, al-though not necessarily precisely what the EWC would have wished. None the less, because of the EWC's European role, the information did go beyond what would have been disclosed at national level. The joint meetings were presided over by the chair of the EWC. The EWC views the joint meetings not only as offering scope for exchanging information but also for raising is-sues of concern to itself and setting out its own views to management.

The annual meetings have so far been the main focus of the EWC's work. Activity between the meetings is looked after by the German works council, which has resources available to it under German law, including an office staffed with specialist and administrative staff.[12] It can use video con-ferencing for internal communication, has access to the company's intranet and even has its own programme on the internal TV station. However, these options have not yet been used for EWC work. The steering committee, which consists of three German members, one French and one Spanish mem-ber, had had only one meeting when our research was carried out, and had not defined its precise functions. At present, the EWC chair and their deputy – both German – determine the direction and pace of the EWC's develop-ment. They view the EWC as an extension of the policies of the German cen-tral and group works councils at European level (a 'fourth tier of co-determination') and see themselves as responsible for the group's foreign employees. As in their domestic activity, they are looking for 'social' solutions to their problems. The attempt to interweave works council work at the group's HQ with the EWC is testified to by the fact that the group works council steering committee is identical to the German delegation on the EWC. The chair of the EWC and group works council feel that, over the longer term, the group works council could be dissolved and replaced by the EWC, and that the EWC itself could evolve into a negotiating body.

European Works Councils in the Insurance Sector

A total of 29 insurance companies in the EU/EEA fall under the EWC Directive. Nearly all these companies have concluded voluntary EWC agreements. As a consequence, and in contrast to banking, insurance is nearly wholly accounted for. All these agreements were made between 1994 and 1996 during the phase of 'enforced voluntarism' – in many cases shortly before the deadline date. In some cases, provisions for an exchange of information between group managements and employee representatives pre-dated the agreements.

The adoption of the Directive in 1994 and Budget line 4004, which enabled a large number of meetings for employee and trade union representatives, provided the momentum to get negotiations in train. The CFDT (France), DAG (Germany), SETCa (Belgium) and MSF (UK) were all particularly active. A large number of agreements were concluded in the wake of these meetings, often with the involvement of Euro-FIET which persuaded managements that voluntary agreements represented a less expensive option than the compulsory negotiations required after September 1996.

The EWC at DBV-Winterthur

The EWC at the Swiss insurance group DBV-Winterthur functions primarily as a forum for the receipt of information from management, which has tended to use meetings as an opportunity to set out its views. Plenary sessions have turned on issues of concern to management, with matters of interest to the EWC, in its view, pushed into the background. Specifically, questions raised by the EWC were either not answered or felt to have been responded to inadequately. The majority of EWC members are not involved in the preparation of the annual meetings. One indicator of this is the fact that, despite requests, the EWC chair has not as yet received any proposals for the agenda from EWC members. Internally, the EWC has not developed any structures for ongoing activity, beyond procedures for electing a chair and deputy.

The development of the EWC has been held back both by the structure of the group, with a Swiss parent company, and the EWC's own internal organisation. Employee representatives at the group's headquarters are not included in the EWC, obstructing local direct access to group management to obtain information and voice EWC concerns.[13] In addition, the German national delegation, which is the largest and which is fully informed on group matters by virtue of German legislation, has little direct interest in developing the EWC. (The 18-strong forum consists of five German representatives, three each from Spain and Italy, two each from France and Belgium, and one each from Austria, Portugal and the Netherlands.) The view of the chair of the German groups works council is telling: the EWC is a 'wafer biscuit with no food value'. Because of a diary clash he and the other German EWC members did not attend the EWC's first meeting. As a consequence, the key positions within the EWC are occupied by employee representatives from smaller national delegations. The chair is Belgian, and the deputy Italian.

Although the establishment of the EWC was initiated by Euro-FIET, negotiations were conducted with the Belgian unions. Euro-FIET obtained a regular seat on the EWC. The development of the EWC was not subsequently pursued with any great energy, with EWC members left largely to their own devices. With no EWC members at the group's headquarters and the absence of the largest and most privileged national delegation, the EWC had no means of 'opening doors' to group management based on existing channels.

However, thanks to the engagement of some individual EWC members from the foreign subsidiaries, the development of the EWC seems to be more delayed than permanently blocked. Interviews with several EWC members showed that the EWC and its members are engaged in a learning process and that its members want to have more influence at the plenary meetings and set up structures for ongoing activity and communication to ensure more continuity, both internally and in contacts with group management. One step in this direction is a proposal to elect a secretariat.

The EWC at Allianz

The EWC at the German insurance company Allianz was still at an early stage of constitution at the time this research was conducted. Only the constitutive meeting had taken place. Opposition from group management meant that an Article 13 agreement was not concluded until shortly before the transposition deadline in September 1996.

However, a precursor body to the EWC had existed in the group since 1981, whose annual meetings were organised and financed by FIET. As a consequence, only union-organised employee representatives could attend. At the last of these meetings, group management paid for the hire of premises and management representatives attended some of the meetings. However, this only entailed giving presentations and responding to questions: they refused to engage in discussion.

Group management was very restrictive in its attitude to requests for participation from the EWC. The process of negotiation and the substance of the agreement mirrored this 'spirit of refusal' (to quote an EWC member). Although management representatives disclose information to the annual EWC meetings to an extent comparable with that supplied to the German 'Economic Committee' *(Wirtschaftsausschuss)* and seek to answer questions in a formally proper way (to 'German standards'), EWC members feel that their need for information is not adequately met. For example, group management – represented by the group European and personnel managers – attended the constitutive meeting for only two hours. Moreover, the presentations largely failed to match the needs of EWC members. Management representatives gave what were, for the EWC members, uninteresting and abstract presentations on company policy (such as rate-of-return targets and developments within individual businesses), with little of value from the EWC's standpoint (such as, criteria for personnel planning and whether these were consistent across Europe). Although the EWC bureau has the right under the agreement to obtain information between meetings and to be consulted on extraordinary matters, a request for this prompted by the announcement of the acquisition of a French insurance company was rejected by management on the grounds that no decision had been reached. Only the two German members of the three-person bureau – not the Spanish member – have access to group-level information between annual meetings through their membership of the company's supervisory board, economic committee and group works council.

Whilst group management does not wish to extend the scope for the EWC's participation beyond information disclosure, it has considered locating some components of pay (and hence a central matter of the respective interests of the company and employees) at the European level through a Europe-wide employee share scheme.

The establishment of an internal operational and communication structure is still in its infancy. As yet not all EWC members have access to electronic means of communication, as had been promised by the company. EWC members have decided to communicate in English to ease internal communications, and some EWC members have begun language courses.

At the instigation of the German delegation, a Spanish member was elected to chair the EWC in order to forestall any concerns about German domination of the body. This implied a conscious acceptance that the work and communications of the EWC would be less efficient, in exchange for securing the longer term development of the EWC as a political project and a European forum. Information is sent in translation to the chair of the bureau and from there forwarded to all EWC members.

Whether the EWC at Allianz will chart a service or project-based course is not yet definitively established. EWC representatives from the foreign subsidiaries have an (initial) interest in drawing on services via EWC representatives at the group's head office in order to be able extract more 'value-added'. However, despite evident efficiency losses, the latter have set in train a process of project-based development. As a consequence, neither of the two paths has been pursued with rigour. Although these are teething troubles which will be overcome in time, there is a danger that EWC members could lose interest if it proves to be inefficient over the longer term.

The EWC at Basler Versicherung

The EWC agreement at the Swiss insurance group Basler Versicherung was negotiated at the company's German subsidiary and signed in September 1996, with the employer side eager to avoid the need to conclude an Article 6 agreement. The 14-person EWC consists of five members from Germany, one each from Belgium, the Netherlands, Luxembourg, Spain, France and Italy, and finally three members from Switzerland (who have 'guest status' and fewer rights). No steering committee was set up; rather the agreement provided for the election of an EWC chair and deputy chair. The chair, a German employee representative from a small subsidiary, is the key figure in the EWC. He has taken responsibility for developing the EWC, and can make use of the resources available through the German codetermination system.

As well has having privileged access to group-level information, in part through membership of the supervisory board, following a complaint about the lack and unsatisfactory timing of information disclosure he was added to the circulation list for management information and since then has been informed in detail, both orally and in writing. As a rule, he forwards information by fax to other EWC members. The EWC chair functions as an information provider and guarantor of the continuity of the EWC between annual meetings. When required, he will intervene in national matters and seek to conciliate, as happened with a planned relocation of a number of posts within the Spanish subsidiary. Only one of the 40 people affected was prepared to move. Thanks to ad hoc negotiations by the EWC chair, redundancies could be avoided for the other 39 employees. This represented a special case as group management evidently welcomed his intervention into what was a politically delicate situation in the context of the wider Basque conflict.

The chair would like to develop the EWC into a more effective body and extend its scope for participation. In this connection, the revision clause in the agreement will offer an opportunity to raise the frequency of employee meetings (whilst retaining the annual rhythm for meetings with group management) and press for a trade union right to participate in meetings. In the longer-term, the chair would like to initiate negotiations with group management to arrive at European-level agreements on issues such as employee share schemes and the health and safety of VDU-based workstations.

The EWC at AXA-UAP

Although the EWC at the French insurance group AXA-UAP fulfils service functions for national employee representatives, its main thrust is towards developing projects, with a clear priority for the building of internal operational and communication structures. The aim here is to strengthen the capacity of the EWC in its dealings with group management. The EWC agreement only provides for modest participation rights. None the less there are elements which offer scope for the EWC to develop its own projects. The EWC has its own budget of FF 500,000 a year. In addition, the company pays for a half-time post for the EWC secretary (the other half being as a full-time official for the CFDT trade union).

The central organising focus is a secretariat, which embraces employee representatives from the group's foreign subsidiaries and is built around an agreed internal division of labour (such as social issues, economic matters, finance). The secretariat meets at different locations between annual meetings. In order to strengthen the effectiveness of the EWC, tailored training has been offered and implemented, including English language courses. There are also proposals to establish a dedicated EWC information network. Procedures for information exchange between EWC members and the secretariat still remain to be developed; as yet, despite requests, EWC members have not submitted information to the EWC. Conversely, the EWC secretary only rarely forwards information unprompted to EWC members. In future, information will be collected and prepared on a more systematic, issue-related, basis. Ideally – and in theory – this would lead to a handbook on 'Terms and Conditions in Europe' (or 'The 35-hour week'), which could be used in discussions with group management.

As yet, the EWC feels that it is not being taken seriously by the company, and would like to be able to counter this with its own information system which would, it hopes, allow it to enter into discussions with management on the basis of a better level of understanding. In the event of serious problems at individual European locations, the EWC offers support to local employee representatives by intervening either at the level of group or local national management. This has happened, for example, in the case of feared job-losses in a Belgian and a British subsidiary.

The merger of AXA-UAP with another French insurance company led to a block on the development of the EWC, which has had to be completely restructured. Employment in the group in Europe rose from 14,000 to 65,000. An EWC already existed in the company with which AXA-UAP merged, although it had not started operations. A straight merger of the two EWCs would have raised the number of members from 29 to over 70. However, group management wanted to cap it at 45. Agreement was eventually reached on 54 members, with the secretariat expanding from four to eight members.

The EWC at AXA-UAP is typical of many EWCs, in which group restructuring has rendered existing arrangements obsolete and served to set back the practical operation of the forum.

The EWC at Victoria

The EWC at the German insurance group Victoria was established in September 1996. Only one annual meeting had taken place by the time this research was conducted. The initiative to establish the EWC was taken by the German group works council, to which group management had responded positively. At its instigation, the central works council of the German parent company had invited foreign employee representatives to works council conferences from 1994. Negotiations on the EWC agreement were conducted by the works council leadership in Germany and the group personnel director. The German EWC representatives organised the annual meeting themselves, sending invitations and setting the agenda, about which they simply informed group management. Even the organisational and technical sides of the meeting were taken care of by the EWC office.

The first joint meeting was attended by the chair and labour director[14] of the group, with individual management representatives participating for specific agenda items. The subjects discussed were the economic situation and strategy of the group, company environmental policy, employment, and employment and social issues (training, health and safety).

An agreement on implementing the requirements of the EC VDU Directive was concluded at the first joint meeting. Like the EWC agreement itself, this agreement was prepared in Germany and 'pre-negotiated': the EWC simply provided the 'official' occasion to conclude it and make provision for its application throughout the group's European operations.

No select committee exists to serve the eight-person EWC (three from Germany, two each from the Netherlands and Austria, and one from Spain). Both the EWC chair and deputy are from Germany. They assume responsibility for preparing and organising meetings, and offer a point of contact. They can also use the German works council infrastructure for EWC work. EWC representatives from the foreign subsidiaries are largely passive and have very little mutual contact. Rather, they have simply delivered complaints to the EWC chair about the behaviour of local managements. In one case, the Spanish member complained about the disclosure of information locally, and an Austrian member raised the issue of the treatment of the works council at national level. In both cases, group management intervened and the works council checked to see whether the complaints were being pursued.

The level of internationalisation of Victoria – with 10 per cent of its employees outside Germany – is fairly low. Individual foreign subsidiaries also have only a few hundred employees. This structure is reflected in the EWC's internal workings. The German EWC representatives view the EWC as a 'fourth tier of co-determination', and their aim is to extend the standards which prevail at the German sections of the group to the European level. The agreement on VDUs represents an exemplary instance of this: although adopted by the EWC, the agreement was made without including EWC representatives from the foreign subsidiaries in discussion and negotiation.

At the time this research was carried out, Victoria was on the threshold of a merger with two other German insurance companies; if carried out it would necessitate a restructuring of the EWC.

Conclusions from the Case Studies

This overview of the 15 case-studies provides an opportunity to develop the four EWC models in our typology by setting them against the practice of real EWCs. This allows a better defined profile of the dynamics of EWC development to be elaborated in accordance with the characteristics of the four models, their developmental preconditions, and the factors which obstruct and facilitate them. Aside from the symbolic EWC, the models embody different priorities and developmental paths for EWCs. In practice, EWCs often encompass the objectives of all three of the active models. Every EWC is confronted with the task of finding the optimal combination from a variety of options and of choosing a path which best fits its own structure and the demands placed on it. Not every EWC can embark on every developmental path. On occasions there may be structural obstacles which can be surmounted, but also barriers which are insurmountable; obstacles can also be rooted in the character, origin and outlook of the individuals concerned.

The Symbolic EWC

Around half the cases in our sample can be classified as symbolic EWCs: these were DBV-Winterthur, Allianz, Bayerische Vereinsbank, Crédit Lyonnais, Kredietbank and Oetker. Their activities are mainly confined to the annual plenary meetings and EWC members are, for the most part, passive between meetings and do not prepare for the plenaries. As a consequence, the meetings serve less to provide information to EWC members than to offer a stage for management to set out its views. In the case of Bayerische Vereinsbank the annual meeting has never lasted more than three hours. Representatives of group management attend and make presentations on corporate culture and the bank's strategic objectives. The course of the plenary meeting at Oetker is illustrative. Group management dominates simply by virtue of numbers, with EWC members obliged to occupy the 'second row'.

Symbolic EWCs have either not yet developed because of the short span of time since their inception or are not amenable to development because of structural factors or issues related to individual employee representatives. Examples of EWCs which have not yet developed are ABN AMRO and Allianz. In both cases, there is sufficient potential to suggest that a rapid advance beyond the symbolic stage is likely. In the case of ABN AMRO, at which only one meeting had taken place at the time this research was conducted, organisational and personal links had been created during the process of establishing the EWC which suggest that it will become project-oriented – a development favoured by the approach to setting up the Special Negotiating Body (SNB) which ensured that EWC representatives were included in decision-making structures at an early stage. This international composition will continue in the future as some of the SNB members will become members of the steering committee.

On the other hand, the case-studies also show that structural obstacles can temporarily prevent an EWC from moving on from the status of a symbolic forum, and may have longer term effects. In particular, groups with a low degree of internationalisation, where the focus of employment and operations are concentrated in the group's home country, and where individual subsidiaries are fairly small offer only poor prospects for EWC development.

The most notable examples of this are Bayerische Vereinsbank and Oetker. EWC contingents from the foreign subsidiaries are weak, both in terms of numbers and access to resources, and as a consequence cannot push forward the development of the EWC. They expect and hope for support from EWC members at the company's home base. Although the latters' circumstances are usually better, they are less dependent on a functioning and effective EWC and can often pursue international concerns via domestic arrangements. This situation can permanently block the development of the EWC should representatives from the home base be unwilling to take on a service role (such as distributing information) for EWC members in foreign subsidiaries.[15]

In the case of Crédit Lyonnais, the situation has hardened to a degree that the development of the EWC is may have become blocked permanently. In fact, during a crisis at the bank, the low level of interest of EWC representatives from the home base culminated in a policy which was directed against EWC members from the group's foreign subsidiaries in that it supported a rationalisation plan which was detrimental to the bank's foreign subsidiaries. As a consequence, the German EWC delegation withdrew.

The Service EWC

Of the 15 case-studies, four – Basler Versicherung, Kredietbank, Deutsche Bank and Allied Domecq – can be assigned to the category of service EWCs. Three types of service can be distinguished.

In the first, individual EWC members forward information to their colleagues between meetings. For example, the two German members of the directorate at the German insurance group Allianz receive a good deal of information between the EWC's annual meetings by virtue of their membership of national representative bodies (supervisory board, economic committee and group works council).[16] This is then forwarded to other EWC members, albeit after a slight delay occasioned by its routing via the Spanish EWC chair. The German EWC chair of the Swiss insurance group Basler Versicherung also has privileged access to information and contact to group management through membership of the company's German supervisory board. In addition, he is also on the circulation list for management information and as a rule faxes information relevant to the EWC to other EWC members.

Secondly, the EWC (at least in the person of the chair) can put problems which occur at local national operations to group management and as a result have what are local or national issues dealt with at a higher level. For example, the EWC chair at the French insurance group AXA-UAP intervened when jobs were under threat at the Belgian and British subsidiaries. The EWC at Kredietbank remained involved during the restructuring of the German subsidiary. This case was discussed by the EWC and its steering committee. Although the final decision was a matter for national management, these consultations strengthened the hand of the German works council in its negotiations since group management had acknowledged that there was scope for local negotiation – something which the German national management had disputed.

Thirdly, individual EWC members (at least the EWC chair and the authority vested in their office) can seek to mediate in national conflicts. One example of this can be seen once more in the case of Basler Versicherung, where the EWC chair had found out from his Spanish colleague that 40 jobs were to be relocated from San Sebastian to Madrid. Although this was theoretically a national issue, he travelled to Spain to mediate on the spot and secure a socially-acceptable solution. In fact, political sensitivities about the Basque conflict meant that group management supported his intervention.

The provision of services by individual members or national delegations implies a 'welfare' role, but also creates a potential for control. This applies in particular where the service provider acts from a position of strength (either based on the strength of the national delegation and/or the resources available through the national system of employee representation). Such a situation can afford an opportunity for individuals or groups to control the direction and pace of EWC development and steer it to suit their own interests. In particular, they can obstruct the emergence of a genuinely supra-national quality to EWCs by occupying and retaining key roles in the forum. Such control can prevent the EWC from developing as a project-oriented forum, as this requires that control should be relinquished and that national contingents be brought into the decision-making process on an equal basis.

There are points of overlap between service EWCs and project-oriented and participative types. For example, service and project-oriented EWCs converge where the EWC as a whole, or its steering committee, is involved in the organisation and delivery of services. This presupposes processes for organisation and decision-making within EWCs, at least within the steering committee. As in the case of Kredietbank, where the EWC was involved in the restructuring of a national subsidiary, the provision of a service can become a consciously-chosen and organised project of the EWC as a whole.

There is also a transitional zone between the service and participative EWC, again with two dimensions. In the first, an EWC will move into a transitional zone should individual EWC members intervene to conciliate or mediate in national disputes, with the prospect of ad hoc negotiations with decentralised local managements. A transition to a participative EWC can also exist if the efforts to provide services made by EWC members are extended by making agreements which previously had only national validity apply at the European-level, thus allowing employees in foreign subsidiaries to benefit. One example of this is the EWC at Victoria.

Project-oriented EWCs

The key question for project-oriented EWCs is that of how they can organise 'everyday business' not via a single national group of employee representatives but via EWC's own structures and, in the best case, using its own resources. This presupposes agreement within the EWC on the tasks and issues to be tackled, just as – conversely – defining and tackling areas of work promotes the establishment of efficient structures for activity, communication and decision-making which include all EWC members. Examples of this type can be seen in the cases of AXA-UAP and Unilever. In the latter case, the EWC developed as an exemplary instance of a project-oriented institution because management's protracted obstructive stance prevented movement towards a participative EWC: since then, however, it has enjoyed a number of 'participative' successes.

The case-studies show that the key decisions which could promote future project-orientation are taken as early as when the EWC agreement is negotiated. In the cases of ABN AMRO and Unilever, EWC negotiations were conducted by a negotiating body on which employee representatives from the foreign subsidiaries were represented: in both cases the core of this body became the EWC's steering committee. Moreover, the agreement itself serves to set the preconditions for the EWC's ongoing work. Examples include scope for separate meetings for the EWC, the formation of a select or steering committee, access to a communications' infrastructure, and independent EWC financial and staff resources.

Development into an effective body, able to take up and balance the interests of national delegations, can represent the first area of activity – or 'project' – for the EWC, thereby creating the internal preconditions for implementing issue-related projects. Where this happens the EWC will need to tackle those internal obstacles rooted in the interests and activities of its members, raise the skills of EWC members (in particular, languages), reduce prejudices and misunderstandings, build internal capacity, and establish procedures for information exchange, and develop mechanisms for reaching internal agreement and making decisions.

The case-studies suggest that the existence of a steering or 'select' committee, functioning as an operating and organising centre for the EWC, constitutes a key precondition for a project-oriented EWC. Such a committee assumes responsibility for conducting the 'everyday business' of the EWC, for taking key initiatives, and for rendering the work of the EWC visible to other EWC members as a political institution engaged in ongoing activity and capable of intervention. This is demonstrated by the project-oriented EWCs at AXA-UAP and Unilever. In the case of the EWC at AXA-UAP, whose steering committee sees itself as responsible for organising the EWC's work and as a support mechanism, the steering committee is responsible for the three areas of social, economic issues and financial matters, with individual committee members responsible for each of these areas.

The extension of the capacity of the EWC through the establishment of its own information system is the key priority for project-oriented EWCs, enabling them to argue their case independently of group management. In particular, such EWCs need to obtain information via their own structures, such as national systems of employee representation. The creation of independent channels of information allows them to obtain information of a different quality, direct from local operations, and uncoloured by or selected on the grounds of the perspective of a single actor (the employer) or of location (corporate headquarters). This also enables them to check the accuracy of information provided by group management (cf. Nagel et.al., 1996, pp. 16ff and 173ff).

EWCs hope to be able to use this to anticipate company policy, develop alternatives to strategies proposed by management, improve their own position in discussions with management and intervene earlier – with a defence – in the event of corporate restructuring.

The establishment of an EWC information system can consist in the systematic collection of basic data on the group, its individual business units and subsidiaries as well as individual operations. Such data would include information on the economic position and development of the group, rationalisation and restructuring measures planned or in train, and changes in employment and terms and conditions. The EWC at Unilever has established a database for this purpose, to which individual EWC members can add information obtained locally.

EWCs can also compile information on particular issues. For example, the EWC at AXA-UAP is considering bringing together information on terms and conditions in the group into a single document. The EWC at Unilever has compiled, with the help of a Dutch consultancy, a handbook on national and local policies and procedures on restructuring in the group, embracing closures, disposals, and job cuts. This handbook is intended to set out the various options available in law and practice, and to include agreements which have been concluded. And in connection with agreements with central management, either proposed or concluded, the EWC at Danone surveyed health and safety, training, and equal opportunities. In all these cases, the EWC relied on the broad and active involvement of its members.

The EWC at Unilever is pursuing more projects which go beyond simply extending the range of information available to it. Firstly, it is developing policy principles to guide the EWC in the event of corporate restructuring. Amongst other things, EWC members have agreed an appropriate relationship between production, marketing and sales in each country and have committed themselves to resist transfers of production from smaller countries. Secondly, the EWC intervenes into the 'public domain' – both within and outside the group – with its own positions. A statement of the EWC's view of the group's European policy is pinned up in all the company's establishments and it intends to hold its own press conference, in the form of a public EWC meeting, on the day that the company holds its press event. Such projects presuppose internal procedures to allow common positions to be developed and agreed.

Project-oriented EWCs can make project outcomes available to national employee representatives in the form of higher quality services. For example, they not only forward information obtained from group management to the national level, but also compile and interpret it, adding information both from central management and individual operations within the group. Not only do individual EWC members intervene in national disputes but the EWC itself makes national disputes into 'its business' and has a distinctive view of them.

There are also a number of points of overlap between project-oriented and participative EWCs. Widening EWC activities poses the question of the resources available to do this, the issue of time-off for EWC or steering committee meetings, issues of financing, and provision of the necessary infrastructure. Project-orientation almost invariably entails raising the question of financing, and with this the need for the EWC to negotiate with group management 'in its own cause'. And if on this, why not on other matters?

Project-orientation can also be primarily aimed at creating the preconditions for participation. In such circumstances, the EWC will concentrate on projects which raise its understanding and capacity to engage with management when differences of interest occur, and those allow the power resources of national employee representatives and/or trade unions to be used by the EWC. In such cases, project-orientation aims at improving the EWC's status and ability to prevail vis-à-vis management.

The Participative EWC

Although several EWCs exhibit a desire to influence specific corporate policies, a 'participative' EWC implies that EWCs seek to extend their scope for involvement on a broader and more systematic basis. On this measure, of the 15 EWCs in the sample, Danone, Nestlé and Deutsche Bank can be assigned to this category. Two forms of participation can be distinguished.

1) The EWC works towards participation in the decision-making process which shapes group-level policy and operations and seeks to open up corresponding channels of influence by institutionalising procedures for timely information and consultation, either on a formalised basis or through custom and practice.

    In the cases of Unilever and Nestlé, procedures for including the EWC in discussions on group-level restructuring measures which have a substantial effect on employees were embodied in the EWC agreement and already been put to practical use. In each case, a select committee serves as the forum for information and consultation. The practice of consultation in these examples highlights two issues. Firstly, there is the fundamental question of *when* information is to be disclosed. Even if the EWC is formally required to be informed prior to a final decision, management may already have long been committed to a particular course. Secondly, consultation offers the prospect of conducting *ad hoc* negotiations (such as measures to mitigate the impact of changes). During consultation, the EWC and the managers responsible will sit across the same table, and the EWC will make proposals to modify measures, to mitigate the social consequences, or negotiate compensation. The cases of Unilever and Nestlé show that EWC negotiators are by no means powerless in this area.

2) The EWC seeks recognition as a negotiating partner and actor in the conduct of industrial relations at group-level by winning the right to negotiate on less conflictual issues and to conclude formal agreements. There may be points of common interest between the EWC and group management on a range of negotiating issues. This applies in particular if management is committed to strategies to promote corporate identity throughout the group. Possible areas of mutual interest include pan-European all-employee share schemes, improvements in health and safety, and the implementation of EU Directives (such as on VDUs) throughout the group.

The case of Danone shows that, given willingness on the part of group management, wide-ranging agreements can be concluded which meet the interests of both parties. The agreements so far are aimed at harmonising decentralised conflict-resolution procedures and obtaining the commitment of national and local managements. This both strengthens trade union rights at local level and widens the scope for access to information on the part of employees and workforce representatives, together with the information and consultation rights of trade union or employee representatives, in the event of workplace changes which might prove detrimental to employment levels or terms and conditions.

Danone, Victoria and Unilever illustrate the various possible developmental paths of participative EWCs. At Danone, spurred on by trade union interest in extending the scope for EWC participation and demonstrating some negotiating successes, and given the openness to negotiation shown by group management, trade union representatives – who dominated the EWC – set out to develop the EWC into a participative body from the outset. It was success in the field of participation that meant that corresponding internal structures and procedures developed almost automatically.

In contrast, the EWC at Unilever took the opposite course, moving from project orientation to seeking greater participation. Given that group management was initially hostile to the EWC, combined with an internal EWC constitution that prevented dominance by any national contingent, the EWC prioritised internal development and capacity building. This allowed it to win the respect of management and become a serious actor in group-level policy.

Finally, the EWC at Victoria trod the path from a service to a participative EWC. The national strength of workplace employee representation together with co-operative industrial relations at the parent company's home base meant that employee representatives at the group's headquarters saw their task as representing the interests of their foreign colleagues. This also included extending agreements with group management to embrace the European level, hence 'Europeanising' national standards. Such a developmental path, which might be dubbed 'parent-company dominated participation', can become problematic if insufficient attention is given to the central interest of foreign EWC representatives in such services (information, concrete support) or if European regulation is not in the interests of employees in foreign subsidiaries (differences of interest, protectionism). However, it can lead to substantial improvements in employment conditions for employees and create scope for activity on the part of employee representatives in foreign subsidiaries.

Prospects

The 15 EWCs in our sample embrace a wide range of EWC practices and dynamics, with a number of distinctive models of development, types of actor and range of activity. One evident fact is that many EWCs have not yet realised the potential which is latent in the institution, and several will not be able to do even over the longer term. As such they have no practical relevance for workforce representation. Those EWCs which have advanced beyond the status of being largely symbolic institutions could also regress. Many EWCs are still unstable and dependent on external support – for practical and policy purposes from the trade unions, on offers of networking, and on further political and legal backing (in the form of a revision of the Directive).

However, there are also a number of EWCs which are striving to move on and which illustrate EWCs' potential for development. Such EWCs are already capable of delivering 'value-added' in the field of employee representation. They support local employee representation (service EWC), and have begun to acquire the status of an actor at group-level by giving opinions (project-oriented EWC), or having to be consulted or engaged in negotiation with group management (participative EWC).

The EWC models set out above illustrate the various stages and states of development and the differing objectives of EWCs. The prerequisites, motives and scope for action of each model place particular demands on trade union support and on the conception and development of EWC networks. For example, whilst training is especially important in the case of symbolic EWCs, this may take a back seat in project-oriented and participative EWCs with their greater emphasis on how the exchange of information, co-ordination and co-operation can extend the reach of employee representation and how EWCs can acquire greater capacity to prevail on issues of employee interests. Specific EWC models will require differing forms of networking and trade union support. The issue of how EWCs are to be integrated with other fields of trade union policy will also differ markedly for project-oriented and participative EWCs as compared with symbolic or service EWCs.

Notes

1   Regulations implementing the Directive came into force in the UK on 15th December 1999: UK-based companies or other undertakings previously not within the scope of the Directive had up until this date to conclude a voluntary agreement under the 1997 'extension' Directive.

2   For a more detailed treatment, see Lecher et.al., 1999.

3   This does not, of course, apply if an EWC is formally included in projects initiated and organised by management but in which it has no real say. The precondition is a recognisable contribution from the EWC.

4   Mutual exchange of resources not only plays a decisive role in this field of interaction but also in general for employee representatives in an international undertaking. From the standpoint of the EWC what is important is the extent to which it succeeds in obtaining resources from group management, the national level and/or the trade unions and, conversely, to deploy its own resources in the interests of national employee representatives and through this secure a European 'value-added' for employee interest representation.

5   The analysis of the constitution of EWCs, as in Lecher et.al. (1999), points to learning processes for EWCs which lend a certain plausibility and empirical support to the view that EWC types can be understood as stages of development.

6   Jointly initiated and implemented projects presuppose processes of negotiation, irrespective of how informal and one-sided they might be. In turn, these are the outcome of discussion and negotiation between the EWC and group management, and as such serve as an indicator for the body's degree of participation – aside from the exception noted above where an EWC may be formally incorporated into a project initiated and organised by management but in which it lacks any genuine consultative rights.

7   This is not coterminous with the food industry for which there is no specific data. Aside from food, the IUF is also responsible for hotels, catering and tourism.

8   Consultation is defined in the Unilever agreement as: 'Exchange of views and establishment of a dialogue. Consultation will take place in the course of the normal decision taking process, where possible, prior to the implementation of the decision and will concern the principles underlying the decision'.

9   To quote the agreement: 'When there is a need for dialogue on transnational issues of major importance, significantly affecting the employees, a Special Committee of the Council will meet between the general meetings of the Council. This consultation should take place as soon as possible when such issues arise, in order not to impede or delay their resolution. After consultation, final decision shall remain with Nestlé management'.

10   The steering committee, which is the counterpart to management between meetings, prepares dossiers on the commercial and financial position of the group for the EWC and deals with ongoing problems. It consists of five Belgian representatives but can co-opt another representative from the country concerned in the event of problems.

11   The EWC at Kredietbank conducts itself in accordance with the customary practice for Belgian employee representatives, as Udo Rehfeldt as described elsewhere: 'In Belgium, works councils do not have information rights on economic matters. In contrast, it is usual for the reasons advanced by management for reductions in employee numbers not to be debated. Rather, any social cushioning for such measures forms the object of negotiations' (Rehfeldt, 1998, p. 456).

12   The establishment of an employee representative office was negotiated in the wake of the EWC agreement. The outcome was not a specific office for the EWC but rather a bureau which improved the infrastructure available to the German group-level works council and strengthened the hand of the German EWC delegation.

13   The EWC Directive treats Swiss undertakings as non-European companies. Irrespective of their registered headquarters, such undertakings fall under the Directive if they meet

the size criteria within the European Economic Area. An Article 13 agreement was concluded without including Swiss employee representatives. Such an agreement was in the interest of the trade unions as they found it difficult to gauge the standpoint of the non-unionised Swiss employees.

14   Under German codetermination requirements, supervisory boards of larger companies must contain a 'labour director' who is responsible for personnel and employment matters and who must enjoy the confidence of employee representatives on the board.

15   Given such a relationship between parent company and subsidiaries, a service orientation might well represent the most appropriate prospect as the low level of resources of foreign employee representatives means that projects can only be engaged in to a limited extent.

16   In fact, the information provision has been so limited as yet, that the EWC at Allianz is in fact assigned to the category of 'symbolic' EWC.

4 Networking EWCs:
Initiatives – Needs – Prospects

Although most EWCs are still engaged in the search for an appropriate strategy on what remains the novel and largely unexplored terrain of European transnational activity – with its associated new tasks and challenges – there are a number of indications, both qualitative and quantitative, to suggest that transnational enterprise-based structures are beginning to emerge and are lending momentum to the Europeanisation of industrial relations.

As far as the formation of cross-border industrial relations are concerned, two developmental paths can be distinguished. The first consists of the emergence of a pattern of enterprise-based arrangements in which EWCs figure as 'islands of European industrial relations' within what is otherwise a sea of nationally fragmented industrial relations systems. The second consists of the emergence of a structure which links or integrates different levels and arenas of European industrial relations. Although such a system would be promoted by the development of EWCs, their role in it would be limited to that of constituting its decentralised component.

The full realisation of this second path – the only one which could be truly be called a system of European industrial relations – would, on our analysis, require the trade unions to take the initiative to build networks between EWCs from different companies.[1] Such networking would drive forward the development of EWC activity by allowing experience to be shared with other EWCs, by lessening the strain on trade union resources, and by holding out the prospect of integrating EWCs into other fields of trade union policy and activity – such as the co-ordination of national collective bargaining within a European framework and the development of sectoral social dialogue.

Networking and Networks: Conceptual Issues

We understand by networks and the construction or emergence of a (social) network the bringing together of previously independent actors with the aim of generating interactions which lead on to processes of exchange, mutual understanding, co-ordination and agreement, and the development of common strategies. In the case at hand, the actors are, firstly, EWCs – constituted and acting within the framework of the employing company – and, secondly, trade unions, which remain organisationally divided and fragmented. Networks would, therefore, cut across national, functional and ideological divisions within the trade union movement, as well as the lines of demarcation which separate workplace and trade union forms of employee representation.

Weyer (1997) sees a common focus in the discourse on networks conducted by different academic specialisms in the:

> attempt to describe a new quality in interactive relationships which cannot be adequately analysed using the classical repertoire of sociology, political science or economics: that is, co-operation rooted in trust between social actors, who – despite pursuing their own interests – also link their actions with those of other actors in such a way that the success of their strategies depends on the success of their partners (and hence on a functioning relationship of co-operation) (Weyer, 1997, p. 53).

Aside from the fact that instead of a 'new quality in interactive relationships' it might be more appropriate to speak of the incursion of specific types of interactive relationships into other fields, we lean towards a 'softer' concept of networking, with more indeterminacy as far as outcomes are concerned. For example, in our view a network is also conceivable in situations in which actors do not make themselves completely dependent on the functioning of the network in making their strategic choices. Rather the key features of a social network are more its character as a process, its openness to development, and the fact that it remains open to appropriate participants – in this case, additional EWCs. Just as the construction of social network is a process with indeterminate outcomes, by the same token the social dynamic within an existing network is one which is in constant flux.

Despite this 'softer' definition of a network, most of the features of a social network identified by Weyer are still relevant in our context.

1) A network is a system of voluntary co-operation between autonomous actors. Its formation cannot be enforced, and depends ultimately on the willingness of the potential participants: it is 'solely a matter for the participants who, on the basis of subjectively rational motivations, build capacities to link with each other and, under appropriate circumstances, establish stable mutual interactions' (ibid, p. 97). In the context of EWCs, the actors co-operate in the expectation of obtaining a 'surplus effect', which can be related on the one hand to improvements in EWC activity, and on the other to a more effective representation of employee

interests through cross-company co-operation and the integration of EWC policies into other fields of trade union activity. Networking is likely to be most successful where incentives are created, interest aroused and the usefulness of networking highlighted. Conversely, the prospects of success will be less where the input of resources – be it time, cost, or physical and psychological effort – constantly rises. Studies of EWC practice show that the resources which can be, or have been, committed to EWC work are typically fairly meagre. This applies both to the employee representation carried out by multiple-office holders who are granted time off, and whose main activity is usually closer to the immediate workplace, and to EWC representatives from foreign subsidiaries, who often have to conduct their work under generally less favourable circumstances. The trade unions also have capacity problems as far as their support for EWCs is concerned.

2)   Actors are autonomous in setting objectives and decision-making and heterogeneous in regard to their orientations and interests, with the latter partly compatible and linkable. EWCs would need to ascertain those areas in which convergent interests might be presumed to exist and to incorporate into networks those actors with a sufficient degree of homogeneity as far as their organisational preconditions, overall approach and interests are concerned. Whether an EWC would gain from participating in a network, and the function of such a network, therefore depends on the stage of development reached by EWCs and the type of EWC involved. In other words, the success of a network rests on a set of preconditions which are an internal function of EWCs.

3)   The social dynamic set in train by the emergence and development of a network is also a function of the individuals involved. Although the participants in a network are usually delegates from an EWC or a trade union, they are also individuals with their own personalities and characteristics (social, communicative, specialist) and varying degrees of commitment. The success of a network rests not only the circumstances of the actors but also of individuals (such as, knowledge of languages, ability to compromise, stamina).

4)   A network is restricted to a limited number of participants who are able to engage in personal communication. Such communication is the precondition for the initiation of a social process. For the same reason, a network cannot be a perfunctory or coincidental association but

requires a certain duration and degree of consistency. However, it is not ultra-stable and will disintegrate if not stabilised through the concrete actions of the individuals involved. 'The [temporary] stability [over time] of social networks which have emerged in this way is based on a consensus of interests of the participating actors which must prove itself repeatedly in everyday activity' (ibid. p. 98). Nonetheless, structures can be established to help in this process. For example, a 'network manager' (or co-ordinator) can be appointed whose task it is to promote and facilitate it. As a consequence, a network is neither wholly unstructured and nor are its structures given from the outside; rather the participants themselves create structures 'by developing rules and shaping them such that the desired positive effects come about' (ibid. p. 74). Such rules can deal with the internal structure of the network, constitute guidelines for co-operation, or consist of a work programme or list of objectives. A technical infrastructure for communications, such as fax, e-mail, or internet, can provide a supporting framework as it necessitates the establishment of procedural rules for exchanging information.

Networks can emerge in two ways. In the first, informal contacts can become sufficiently massified for a network to develop at the centre, with less dense interaction as one moves to the periphery. That is, a concentration of informal contacts leads to the creation of a stable core, which maintains constant contact and consolidates itself into a pattern of interaction, with scope for a variety of other actors to join and leave. In the second, one or several clearly defined and demarcated networks (possibly even entailing formal delegation) could be created through a deliberate process. In view of the fact that EWCs are still at an early stage of development, the first path would seem to be the more promising. None the less, the lack of resources available to the actors could oblige them to adopt a more purposive approach.[2]

A network, therefore, signifies much more than meetings held at greater or lesser intervals. It lives from the self-organisation of the participants – together with the fact that this sets in train a social dynamic. Contact, initially prompted externally, generates a growing density of informal and autonomous exchange. The network then consolidates and stabilises itself through the use made by the participants of the new possibilities it offers to meet their needs, in turn promoting further network development.[3]

Networks are susceptible to three particular hazards. Firstly, it is in the nature of networks to shield themselves from the outside, and close themselves off socially. Indeed, this is virtually a prerequisite for generating their characteristic internal dynamics. However, such closure can lead to the emergence of new power blocs, with undesirable side-effects. For example, an EWC network which excludes trade unions could undermine existing collective agreements. The exclusion of smaller companies or groups – or employee representatives from groups without an EWC – could reinforce the division between the relatively favourable terms and conditions of employees in large businesses and those employed under less favourable circumstances or in smaller companies.

Secondly, new internal relationships of dominance could emerge and existing relationships of sub- and superordination be multiplied. An EWC network could reproduce the dominance of the parent company in a group, leading to national dominance or the domination of a network by trade unions. Neglecting the interests of EWC representatives from subsidiaries could lead to the fact that, although the EWC network functions as a whole, not all EWCs within the network do so. This is particularly problematic if the network is installed solely at national level.

Thirdly, the formation of networks necessarily leads to a shift of resources which, given their scarcity, can lead to conflicts of interest. Networks that link EWCs are always faced with the problem of the limited resources of the potential participants. This applies as much for full-time trade union officials as it does for any EWC members involved: in the latter case, they may already be vulnerable to the criticism that they have distanced themselves too far from their grass roots, from the workforce and from local issues.

This aside, networks can, and this is their key advantage, set in train a highly productive social dynamic with unintended and unpredictable results. They link a large number of individuals in an active way and allow them scope for initiative and the creation of structures to meet the challenges they face. As a consequence, networks may well represent the best organisational form for linking enterprise and multi-enterprise structures of employee representation. They can mobilise large numbers of individuals, helping to offset the scarcity of trade union resources. And by means of practical activity and in a step by step way which respects the diversity of network participants, they have a particular capacity to develop structures that can bridge the gaps created primarily, although not exclusively, by the differing systems of industrial relations in which they are anchored.

External Reference Points

The prospects and options for EWC networks can only be realistically gauged by considering the preceding quantitative and qualitative stage of

EWC development and current initiatives to link EWCs. Such 'docking points' – existing or potential – consist of a variety of phenomena: for example, unsystematic informal contacts, which might mature into a network over time, existing national initiatives, whose structures and experiences could be drawn on, needs and approaches which have already been articulated and which could be adopted and developed, or existing structures and activity of the European trade unions, in which EWC work could be rooted.

The case studies in this and the preceding volume (Lecher et.al., 1999) have demonstrated that there is a considerable need for EWC networks. However, as yet, such initiatives are very modest in scale. In view of this lack of activity and structure, trade unions now have an opportunity to set about the systematic building of union-based networks, beginning with existing initiatives, and the interests and awareness of potential participants.

Trade Union Support and Networking in the Food Industry

Company-based international trade union activity by the international trade secretariat in the food industry, the International Union of Food, Agricultural, Hotel, Restaurant, Catering, Tobacco and Allied Workers Unions (IUF), extends back to the early-1970s with efforts to establish 'world company councils' in a number of internationally-operating businesses. However, not least because of the absence of external stabilisation, such councils – initiated, financed and organised by the IUF – mostly failed to endure. Regular meetings only took place up until the late-1970s.

These experiences were available to the IUF and ECF-IUF when the first voluntary EWCs were agreed. (ECF-IUF is the European Committee of Food, Catering and Allied Workers' Unions within the IUF: it was formed in 1981 out of a merger of the unions represented on the European Committee of Food, Catering and Allied Workers Unions, which was confined to EC states, and the European section of the IUF, which embraced all of Western Europe. The aim was achieve a consistent approach in Europe and internationally. On background, see Stöckl (1986), pp. 193ff.) The IUF and its national affiliates took over the establishment and development of these EWCs, which they saw as an instrument for practical trade union activity at group-level. The adoption of the EWC Directive in 1994 led to a transfer of responsibility for the establishment and practice of EWCs to the ECF-IUF. By 1996 fewer than 10 EWCs had been established within the ECF-IUF's scope: the limited number meant that co-ordination could be managed via personal links (EWC support was delivered by IUF- and ECF secretaries and individual representatives of national affiliates all of whom knew each other).

This situation changed once the pace of EWC establishment accelerated during the Article 13 phase. During this period the ECF-IUF concentrated on maximising the number of EWCs in operation, and in particular on securing its involvement in negotiations and winning agreement on continued participation in EWCs. The ECF-IUF did not delegate the initiation and negotiation of agreements to its local affiliates but tackled the issue centrally. This placed great pressures on ECF-IUF secretaries. Success also meant that the previous method of supporting EWCs was no longer tenable. As a consequence, an approach was developed which entailed the closer involvement of the national affiliate unions. Each EWC is allocated a national trade union for support, and a representative of each trade union serves as a co-ordinator. Co-ordinators meet once a year to share experience, evaluate their work and co-ordinate positions. The ECF-IUF is responsible for co-ordinating between both trade unions and companies. This takes place at trade union level, with no involvement from workplace employee representatives. EWC representatives from individual companies only meet at European level at trade union seminars.

Parallel to EWC activities, additional structures for co-operation and agreement on policy positions exist in a number of branches. Several branch-level committees have been set up under the aegis of the ECF-IUF and operate in the meat, drinks, fish, tobacco, baking, coffee and sugar industries. These consist of representatives of national trade unions affiliated to the ECF-IUF and trade union workplace EWC representatives. Branch committees serve to initiate sectoral social dialogue or – where this is already successfully operating – to arrange for information exchange, policy co-ordination, and the development of common strategic objectives and approaches. For example, there is a European conference in the dairy industry which meets every two years and includes EWC representatives. At the most recent meeting, the discussion revealed a general trend towards higher skill levels in the industry and to more overtime working. One consequence was a commitment by participants to a programme to cut overtime working through national-level action within the context of collective bargaining and by tackling company policies.

Within the food industry, social dialogue is also at sub-sectoral level, with examples so far in the sugar and tobacco industries. The ECF would like to establish committees in the dairy and brewing industries but, as yet, the employers have blocked progress.

The ECF-IUF is eager to co-ordinate both the policy and practice of collective bargaining at European level. Compiling a register of terms and conditions of employment (at branch level) in individual countries is seen as playing an important role in this. This is intended to assist in comparing national collective bargaining outcomes at branch and company level. The initial focus is intended to be on the qualitative aspects of collective bargaining. In view of management attempts to decentralise collective bargaining to group-, company- or workplace-level, the IUF and ECF see a need for bargaining co-ordination between companies to prevent divisions arising between workforces who might then be played off against each other. Such an initiative would place EWCs, as the main actor at group level, at the heart of trade union efforts to co-ordinate bargaining – and would mean that EWC approaches and activities would acquire a key role within trade union strategies. For the ECF, EWCs have a co-ordinating role on quantitative bargaining issues and an active role on qualitative issues.

The IUF and ECF intend to set up a company database which could serve as an important component in any cross-company infrastructure. Amongst other things, it would include the ongoing reporting of EWC activities and a company archive. The preparation and accessing of relevant information, both on companies and EWC activities, would take place via national trade unions. Unionised employee representatives would also have access to the database, although only via the trade unions.

Both strands – EWC and sub-sectoral activity – could be strengthened by a substratum of EWC networks which could integrate workplace employee representatives more strongly into union activity. This would require the formation of corresponding EWC networks at sub-sectoral level, a development which would accord with the need expressed by many EWC representatives for information at the level of the particular branch in which they operate. However, the preconditions for this would first need to be created within the EWCs themselves through the formation of branch committees or at least the allocation of appropriate responsibilities. As yet, attempts to establish such committees have not proved to be successful – primarily because of the refusal by companies to make finance available.

At national level there is a diversity of EWC networks of highly variable quality and organisation which could be turned to and built upon. As a rule, however, there is no such structure for EWC co-operation. Rather, EWC members meet in the context of national arrangements for employee representation which provide opportunities for cross-company contact (such as trade union work or working parties of workplace employee representatives spanning individual employers). We briefly consider a few examples here.

In the *Netherlands*, workplace employee representatives in multinational enterprises are networked both at multi-sectoral level and within the food industry. Although trade unions are included in the sectoral network, the key roles are occupied by workplace employee representatives who determine the issues for discussion. Dutch employee representatives view the positive experience gained from this network as a possible model for networking at European level. One Dutch employee EWC representative proposed at the review seminar held in connection with this study that EWCs themselves should take the initiative and establish a contact group of EWC representatives in the European food industry.

In *Germany*, EWC representatives maintain contact through union structures, and in particular through branch-level collective bargaining committees *(Tarifkommissionen)*. Early in 1998, at the instigation of a number of EWCs, the food and catering workers' union, NGG, established a working party of works councils in the food industry. This body, which meets twice a year, consists of EWC representatives and full-time union officials. Initially intended to facilitate the exchange of information, the forum also serves to help employee representatives develop common positions and agree on policy issues and procedures over the medium term. The working party includes EWCs from the key companies in the sector (which includes tobacco as well as food).

In *France*, contacts between EWC representatives are divided along the political lines of demarcation which separate the main trade union confederations. The French union CFDT does not seek to operate a network purely for EWCs and includes all levels and types of employee representative body. On European issues, the union has set up training and offers opportunities for information exchange.

The ECF-IUF views the EWC as an institution which can help strengthen employee representation at European level and wishes to develop EWCs in a more participative direction. It is generally open to the idea of networking EWCs. This is not surprising as – given its strong position in strategically significant EWCs – it can safely assume that it would not be bypassed by such a network. The ECF-IUF favours a diversity of negotiating levels and arenas. It does not lay great store by uniform structures but rather seeks to bring different policy arenas together through common aims and approaches.

The ECF-IUF recognises the need to draw EWCs from the large and strategically important groups more tightly into trade union activities, to align the issues and objectives of EWC policy, and to locate them within an overall political perspective. This goes hand in hand with the growing confidence of EWC representatives who no longer wish to manage their external links solely via the trade unions but want to establish direct links – although not wishing to cast doubt on their union loyalties. Such an interest can be seen in the initiative, noted above, to establish an EWC working party to cover the scope of the German food workers union NGG, but also in the idea for setting up an EWC committee at European level which could check to see what laws and custom and practice exist to cushion the impact of restructuring and make proposals for European-level harmonisation. To some extent, however, the greater confidence of workplace EWC members is also leading to changes in power relations within EWCs. In addition, EWCs in smaller groups tend to lead a more marginal existence. Representatives from these EWCs are primarily concerned with the development of the EWC itself and do not usually call for outside assistance to do this. The ECF-IUF and its affiliated unions therefore need to ensure that it can offer such representatives scope to break out of their isolation.

Trade Union Support and Networking in Insurance

Euro-FIET played a key role in the establishment of voluntary agreements in the insurance sector, both by initiating EWCs itself and supporting national initiatives. Contacts were made with other trade unions and meetings of workplace and trade union employee representatives within a multi-national group organised under EU budget line 4004. Using the argument that voluntary agreements would be less expensive than the more complex procedures of Articles 5 and 6 of the Directive, officials were able to persuade managements to conclude a number of voluntary agreements. In the overwhelming majority of cases, Euro-FIET was also actively involved in the negotiations.

However, financial and personnel constraints led it to withdraw from active support for ongoing EWC activity and transfer responsibility to national trade union support structures. The fact that national structures also remain for the most part at an early stage of development has meant that, with a few exceptions, EWCs in the sector do not receive adequate trade union support. This is due not least to the fact that Euro-FIET has not yet devoted attention to building up and co-ordinating national trade union support structures.

The status of Euro-FIET, located between FIET as a world organisation and national membership trade unions, does not appear to have been resolved within the organisation. (Since January 2000 FIET and Euro-FIET have been part of Union Network International, whose regional organisation for Europe is uni.europa). Euro-FIET has not had its own European structure but has been directly integrated – both in organisational and personnel terms – into overall FIET structures. Although Euro-FIET has operated its own office in Brussels, this has only been used for lobbying and contacts. FIET's political secretaries were responsible for all the world's regions, including Europe.[4] In their view, the 70 per cent of their time spent on the European region as result of their involvement in the establishment of EWCs was too great and detracted from time available for other regions: they wanted to cut it to 25 per cent.

The role of Euro-FIET, interposed between FIET and the national unions, corresponds to that of EWCs, which occupy the ground between the national level of employee interest representation and world company councils. FIET has wanted to develop EWCs into such bodies, on the ground that banking and insurance are global activities.

Sectoral social dialogue is only weakly developed, and as yet has not gone beyond an agreed definition of issues on which external studies will be commissioned (employment, vocational training). However, FIET could not reach agreement with the three employers' associations on evaluating the results of the studies.

There are few initiatives in the field of networking EWCs at European level. At most, some EWC representatives have used the opportunity provided by FIET meetings to make informal contacts. One starting point might be FIET's Internet project, which gives EWC representatives from different companies access to EWC information. This project aroused great interest on the part of the EWC representatives since it would allow them to share information on EWC best practice.

Networking structures at national level are also at a very early stage of development. Contacts with members of other EWCs are sporadic and informal, where they exist at all. With a few exceptions, no training has been offered by trade unions at national level for EWC members; such events still represent an organisational framework for initial contacts. In France, the CFDT has established a commission for its members who sit on EWCs which meets every six weeks.

Our research found that EWC representatives viewed this situation as unsatisfactory and indicated that they wanted more exchange across companies with greater integration between EWC and trade union activity. They warned about the hazards of 'stewing in your own juice' as this both slowed down the pace of development and impeded the necessary co-ordination with trade unions. Although EWC representatives did not expect a great deal of FIET and its member unions – in the light of past experience and recognition of their limited resources – they felt that steps to overcome the isolation of EWCs had to be initiated and sustained by the trade unions. As a consequence, most of their proposals and demands were directed at the trade unions. (They also stressed the importance of establishing personal contacts with EWCs in other companies, for which the review conference held in connection with this study offered an opportunity. Seminars and conferences also offer scope for making contacts.) Trade unions were expected to distribute EWCs' proposals for networking, and compile and prepare information of relevance to EWCs. In addition to creating an electronic information network, it was also suggested that Euro-FIET should issue a regular bulletin, possibly with EWC involvement in its production.

Given the limited capacity of Euro-FIET, for reasons already outlined above, the fact that EWC representatives expected support from the trade unions stood in stark contrast to the view held by union officials that the time devoted to European work should be trimmed. As a consequence, it is unlikely that EWCs will be integrated into broader union European structures and policy-making at European level. This situation carries with it the danger that EWCs will end up by feeling let down by the trade unions, retreat to a more narrow focus, and remain isolated within their corporate confines.

Trade Union Support and Networking in Banking

As in the insurance sector, Euro-FIET was heavily engaged in the establishment of EWCs in banking, but – for the reasons cited above – withdrew from support for existing EWCs and delegated this task to its national affiliates. However, as yet national support structures are not sufficiently developed to be cope with these demands in full, and sectoral social dialogue has not advanced beyond informal discussions with the three employer associations.

Networking at European level is minimally developed. The training and seminars organised by FIET offer those EWC representatives involved some scope for mutual exchange, although the contacts are intermittent and unsystematic. FIET's Internet project, which will embrace the entire financial services industry, will also allow EWC representatives from the banks to make information available to each other.

EWC members have responded to the lack of trade union support at European and national level in two ways. Firstly, they have registered their need for both training and strategic direction. Euro-FIET has been called on to retain and expand its training programme, matched by corresponding seminars for EWCs at national level. They have also called for training and information exchange to be more attuned to the needs and resources of EWC members from subsidiary companies. Secondly, EWCs have sought to offset the lack of trade union support by taking action themselves. This has included establishing direct contact with other EWCs and making available existing experience in setting up EWCs (such has how to negotiate an agreement) and in managing ongoing activity (for example, by comparing agendas).

At national level there are also a number of instances of co-operation between workplace employee representatives from different companies which offer a basis of experience on which EWC members can draw in developing their own networking.

For example, works councils in the *German* mortgage bank sector have co-operated at national level for some years. This takes the form of a working party, the chair of which serves as a point of contact and is responsible for information exchange. The decision to share texts of workplace agreements has led to a degree of uniformity in provisions throughout the sector.[5] Based on this experience, there has been a call for an EWC network at European-level to develop a number of model agreements which, when tailored to the circumstances of individual companies, could be used as a basis for negotiations with management. Such a network would undoubtedly place new demands on participants' time. For example, meetings would need to take place at more frequent intervals than the annual EWC plenary and meetings would need to be well-prepared. Draft agreements could possibly be compiled in workshops.

In the *Netherlands*, workplace employee representatives from the large banks meet in two bodies for co-ordination between companies. The first exists at multi-sectoral level, and the second at sectoral level. The multi-sectoral forum consists of both employee and employer representatives from large international groups and meets four times a year. Participation is voluntary and both the meetings and forum itself are professionally organised. There is an executive, which meets every six weeks, and a secretariat which supports it. Meetings of the forum last for one day. The agenda is compiled by the executive based on ideas forwarded from company level. The meetings are less aimed at yielding action than in helping in the development of common positions on issues such as employment, the environment, and other relevant topics. The main results are made public. Group management at the company hosting the session takes responsibility for clarifying any joint standpoint to parliament or the public more generally. Conversely, government may invite representatives of the forum to give evidence at hearings.

The second framework for concertation is an inter-bank forum. This is an employee-only body which meets three times a year and has an executive responsible for internal communication and organisation. Trade unions are also invited to the meetings. The main topics of discussion are terms and conditions of employment. Meetings can culminate in bargaining claims which are then developed jointly with the trade unions. However, the forum does not constitute an independent body with its own policies and positions.

During the review conference which followed our research, a Dutch employee representative suggested that comparable national networks could be established in other countries, and networked at European level: that is, national structures could be used to create a transnational structure, with at least one representative per country attending meetings at European level.

In contrast to the insurance sector, the organisation of structures and con-tacts linking EWCs in banking offers a realistic option for offsetting the lack of trade union support. This might begin with ad hoc contacts between EWCs on a needs basis and extend to strategic networks, aimed at raising local em-ployee representatives capacity to engage successfully with managements. Trade unions would only have an auxiliary role in such a structure.

Options for EWC Networks

Three types of network can be distinguished in terms of their functions, based on the actual state of development of EWCs and the prospective demands on arrangements for employee representation at European level. Each represents a set of options for activity and perspectives for development. They are:

1) Good practice networks

2) Project networks

3) Action networks

Good Practice Networks

Study of EWC practice demonstrates the difficulties encountered in advanc-ing beyond the status of the 'symbolic' EWC and how critical these first steps can prove in shaping subsequent development. EWC activity is rife with un-certainty. Established national procedures and approaches cannot simply be transferred to the EWC realm. For workplace representatives and trade un-ions, setting up an EWC means entering a relatively open and unstructured terrain, and brings with it the responsibility for building the capacities needed to operate successfully. Aside from the Directive itself, as transposed into na-tional law, guidance can be found in the practical experience of those EWCs which are already functioning and in trade union approaches to EWC work. As a consequence, sharing experience becomes a vital activity.

A 'good practice' network can serve to facilitate such exchanges. By transferring know-how and knowledge it can help raise the skills and lower the workload of network members. Its primary role is to strengthen the oper-ation of EWCs within enterprises. However, it can (and ought) to encourage the development of activity embracing EWCs from different companies. Such exchanges across company boundaries can help EWCs and trade unions structure, and develop standards for, this new terrain of representation. Sharing good practice embraces three areas.

Know-how on how to set up and operate an EWC

This includes developing answers to a number of strategic questions, such as:

*   How can resources be mobilised for EWC work?
*   How should organisation and communication be structured internally?
*   What scope for participation do EWCs have and how can it be extended?
*   What issues should EWCs tackle on their own account and how should trade union support for EWCs operate and be organised?

It would include issues such as dealing with language differences, differing styles of politics and systems of industrial relations. Practical experience has already been gathered on all these matters and could be made available to other EWCs as both guidance and help.

Good practice in relation to national systems of industrial relations

This would include, for example:

*   the possibility in the French system of works councils having their own budget, and making this into a negotiating aim for EWCs,
*   the advantages – and possibly in the event of insensitive action – the disadvantages of the strong position of trade unions as full members of EWCs, as characterises the Italian situation,
*   British trade unions have much experience in providing advice and guidance in situations where collective bargaining is highly decentralised: the relationship between full-time officials and workplace union representatives (such as shop stewards) might also be instructive, in both a positive and negative sense.

The practice of trade union work on EWCs at national and sectoral level

Work with EWCs, and the accelerating pace of the Europeanisation of trade union activity associated with this, also represents fresh ground for the trade unions. Varying strategies have been pursued at national and sectoral level, with a variety of practical approaches, depending on the union concerned.

Moreover, the practical experience of EWC activity – both in terms of duration and quantity – also varies considerably from union to union.

A good practice network entails a fairly low level of commitment. It is in essence an information turntable: network participants add their experience, knowledge and know-how and draw on that of the other participants. The broader the range of participants, the greater the network's resources. Experience from a variety of sectors and countries would need to be made available to the network in the form of individuals as well as in the form of accessible information. A good practice network is not a closed circle but rather a loose association of all those capable of contributing to the development of EWC practice: that is, practitioners and experts from a variety of sectors and countries, EWC members (as 'experts in their own cause'), trade union officials with EWC responsibilities, and professional EWC advisers (lawyers, accountants, industrial relations specialists). It could also embrace all those with a relationship to EWC activity, such as union officials with internal EWC responsibilities, as well as officials engaged in the external representation of EWCs (such as political lobbying and public relations).

A good practice network serves as a loosely-linked meta-network with more strongly-linked sub-networks – a network of networks. It would also contain a number of elements, some of which are already in existence and some of which still need to be developed, which could gradually accrete into a network. The examples of existing initiatives are taken from our study, which is of necessity selective (individual sectors, countries and EWCs).

1) *Direct experience sharing between EWCs*
   Spontaneous contacts between EWCs enable know-how to be shared. However, as yet there are few indications of more regular contacts, and certainly no consolidated formal structures. The one possible exception is the Netherlands where workplace employee representatives from different companies co-operate in an organised way.

2) *Trade union seminars and meetings*
   These constitute the central framework for cross-company exchanges of information. The level of activity varies by country and sector. EU Budget line 4003/4 was often used for financing. Trade union training is central element in a good practice network: it organises inter-company contacts which over time could consolidate into sub-networks.

3) *Networks of trade union EWC support officials*
   Like EWC representatives themselves, union officials entrusted with

supporting EWCs are also strangers on an unknown terrain. For many, the international dimension is entirely new and often requires additional training in languages, knowledge of different industrial relations systems, and political styles and cultures. There is also uncertainty about the development of the institution of the EWC itself. As a consequence, trade union support structures must facilitate experience sharing between the individual officials involved – possibly in the form of evaluation meetings, as already happens in the food industry.

4) *Advisory networks*
   Those involved in research into EWCs and the professional training and advising of EWCs should also be networked in order to exchange experiences and prevent duplication of effort.

5) *Inter-trade union structures for experience exchange*
   This concerns in particular setting up working groups of national full-time officials on such issues as legal matters, business or management problems, and EWC training. (Some related initiatives have been taken at ETUC/ETUI level but were in abeyance.) Such a network would be necessary and important for the development of a trade union perspective on Europeanisation, and how EWCs should fit into it.

6) *Development of an IT infrastructure*
   The Internet could constitute a helpful platform for disseminating the practical experience of EWCs and trade unions. Both the ECF-IUF and Euro-FIET are developing company databases.

Trade unions evidently have a crucial role to play in initiating and organising good practice networks; in fact, such networks are difficult to imagine in isolation from them. The greatest problem in this respect is where EWCs become trapped within the confines of their own companies, with their experience and knowledge denied to a wider network. At present many EWC members do not see the importance of generalising from and sharing both good and bad experiences. What will be crucial will be how the individual elements of a good practice network become linked. Linkages could be in the form of media (electronic networks, external and public relations), or broad working groups and projects. Trade unions might well play a vital role in lending durability to such groups or projects.

There is a positive mutual relationship between the development of EWCs and networks. Whilst the development of EWCs is advanced by being incorporated in a good practice network, for their part EWCs constitute a zone of learning which can promote the formation and development of European networks. EWC members acquire linguistic competencies and begin to develop an understanding of other systems of industrial relations and political styles, competencies indispensable for the networks that we set out below.

Project Networks

A project network is not simply a turntable for redirecting information and sharing experience but also a structure with its own activities. It is rooted in the emergence of an awareness of common problems and a common interest in developing solutions. A project network may define it own tasks or be instituted for a specific purpose. Since its aim is to deliver a specified set of outcomes, the demands placed on the participants are correspondingly higher than in good practice networks. A project network calls for more reliability, commitment and a focused approach from its participants. It aims to reduce the uncertainties of those involved – and raise their strategic capacities.

Project networks are not focused on individual companies but on sectors or sub-sectors. They enable common problems and issues to be tackled jointly and allow the results to be made available to all the network's participants.

One initial and obvious issue is that of charting the situation and development of the (sub-)sector itself, as a pre-requisite for locating firms and their strategies. This requires the compiling, aggregating and interpreting of economic and employment data about multi-national enterprises and their divisions by tapping into the company knowledge of EWC representatives and possibly external experts. This would allow EWCs to make a more realistic assessment of 'their' group or division's status in the market and its competitive position and to deal with the issue of the future of individual plants or businesses on the basis of more solid information. Information on proposed, or implemented, restructuring measures could also be compiled: this might help in anticipating strategic turning points (and identifying alternatives).[6]

The preconditions for this are that, firstly, the EWCs in the key companies in a branch are networked and, secondly, that the trust between network participants is sufficient to ensure that what might be sensitive information is disclosed to 'the competition'. A realistic and informed assessment of company policies which such a network would allow could enable EWCs to take a more active role in corporate restructuring.

Similar considerations apply to approaches to technical matters, work organisation and corporate structures which are often implemented at different times in different companies. Knowledge sharing about their effects on employees, and the scope for organising defensive measures, would open the possibility of initiating learning processes – avoiding the need for EWCs to reinvent the wheel each time. An exchange of company-level agreements – already practised at national level – would have a similar effect.

Social, employment and environmental issues could also be the subject of a project network. Examples might include responses to management employee involvement strategies, implementing the Directive on environmental audits via EWCs, and policies on outsourcing or mergers. The aim would be to enable network participants to develop a position on these issues, drawing on experience in other companies and contributions from other participants. In addition to these corporate issues, there would also be sectorally specific topics, such as the development of a common position on genetic modification in the food industry or the impact of the euro on financial services.

Finally, a project network could also embrace collective bargaining issues. Relevant information might be compiled on terms and conditions in different countries and companies and presented in a form which would allow for comparison and the transnational co-ordination of national bargaining.

The current state of development of EWCs suggests that there is a need to build project networks and, in view of the initiatives taken so far, that this is feasible and realistic.

Employees evidently share common problems within a sector or subsector and networks would offer scope to tackle issues jointly. For example, employees in the financial services industry reported the following problems which run across company and national borders:

- cuts in company benefits,
- cuts in employee numbers and demergers of business areas,
- longer working hours,
- increase in the proportion of pay accounted for by performance-related elements or payment-by-results.

Employees in the food industry noted the following common issues:

- corporate restructuring and greater competition,
- jobs cuts and reductions in benefits,
- higher incidence of overtime working.

The issue of international corporate restructuring is a central concern in the sectors covered by this study. This is also directly linked with the restructuring of sectors and sub-sectors. The new shape of companies (focus on core business, higher degree of internationalisation) is being attained through mergers, acquisitions and disposals – that is, via measures which embrace several companies. Evaluating group strategy and policy therefore entails looking beyond the confines of the individual employer and considering the broader sectoral context. (EWC representatives at the review conference held in connection with this study expressed a need for such information.)

The trade unions also have an interest in building project networks in order to fill the gaps in information which handicap the co-ordination of collective bargaining. Finally, there are a number of plausible foundations on which such activity could take place. One example would be the branch committees of the ECF, which are already pursuing the objectives described here for project networks. Such committees could be underpinned and supported by branch-specific EWC networks. In some countries there are already issue-based working groups in which both workplace employee representatives and full-time trade union officials are involved: in the scope of the German foodworkers' union, for example, there is a working group on genetic engineering. In the Netherlands workplace employee representatives from the big banks meet with trade union representatives to discuss issues of relevance to employees, with the results feeding into bargaining claims.

Action Networks

Compared with the preceding two types of network, action networks have the widest scope and entail the greatest commitment. They not only serve to strengthen company-level EWC activity, but also allow for interests to be aligned and aggregated. The network itself becomes an active element by synchronising action and co-ordinating positions on relevant issues with the aim of strengthening the capabilities of employee representation at its various levels (EWC, network, trade union).

The high level of commitment required also has implications for the work of EWCs themselves. Participants in the network pledge themselves to common aims and procedures. For EWC members, this means that they must be in a position to speak for and decide on behalf of their entire EWC. Such a mandate will rest either on a pattern of dominance within the EWC or presupposes internal mechanisms for agreeing policies and delegating authority – as described above for the project and participative EWC.

In the following we outline some possible areas of activity for an action network.

In the first place, EWCs could act as lobbyists in their own cause. Examples might include any future revision of the EWC Directive, employee rights under the European Company Statute or other Directives which touch on issues of concern to employees. Such a network could be organised across sectoral and national boundaries, adding to the force of any proposals. It is also conceivable that lobbying could be conducted at sectoral level, for example on a legal structure for genetic engineering in the food industry.

One further area of activity might consist in agreeing potential negotiating issues for EWCs, with the aim of concluding 'lead settlements' to create precedents. The next step might involve parallel demands in several companies or even simultaneous negotiations. (The ECF-IUF regards this as realistic scenario. It could also envisage negotiating on behalf of several EWCs.)

Furthermore, the network could aim at promoting social dialogue at sectoral level, either by calling for dialogue to be initiated or by raising its own demands within the framework of existing social dialogue arrangements.

An action network takes its shape principally from a prior analysis of unmet needs. At present, there are few indications that such networks are an immediate prospect. However, a number of the EWC representatives interviewed in the course of this research, who demonstrated an inclination towards strategy and an awareness of the political realities of EWC work, did express an interest in establishing an action network.

Trade unions are understandably ambivalent about action networks. On the one hand, such networks could offer an opportunity for them to overcome the 'company isolation' of project-based and participative EWCs and integrate these into other fields of trade union activity. Given that EWCs are potential collective bargaining actors, there is a need to align EWC policies with national and sectoral approaches and to integrate these into a co-ordinated European bargaining strategy. In addition, an action network could promote the development of sectoral social dialogue – which, with few exceptions, has barely got started. The employers' side, in particular, has exhibited little interest in conducting such dialogue and using it as a means for regulating industrial relations at European level. A strengthening of structures on the employee side could put pressure on the employers to organise themselves and enter into dialogue with the trade unions.

On the other hand, trade unions are concerned that they might lose control over such a network. EWCs are currently the most dynamic pole in the establishment of European industrial relations. Just as participative EWCs might have a tendency to withdraw into their employing company, so an action network could detach itself from the trade unions and constitute a new power centre. Such a 'decoupling' could present less of a danger in the food industry, but could be a problem in financial services where the structures for trade union support are much weaker. In particular, there are a number of

EWC representatives in the larger banks who would move to take matters into their own hands should the trade unions fail to take the initiative.

The strength of an action network would be directly correlated with the strength and capacity of the EWCs which make it up.

Prospects

We have distinguished three types of network, depending on their function. At the core of good practice networks is the sharing of experience by network participants in order to develop and refine their EWC work. In a project network, participants work towards a joint objective which benefits the work of all. In an action network, the network itself initiates activities, and as a result attains the status of an actor.

This analytical ordering also corresponds with the dynamics of development of such networks. The demands placed on the network and its participants – in terms of internal EWC prerequisites, resources, degree of commitment – steadily increase as we move from a good practice, through a project network to an action network. In the first instance, the network functions as a 'turntable'. Participants submit their experiences and draw on the experience of others. In the second case, the network functions as a 'producer'. The participants bring information, experience and knowledge to the network, work on them together, and produce additional knowledge which they can use for their own 'local' work (including agreement on joint action by the participants). In the third case, the network itself functions as an actor. Participants align their interests sufficiently to allow joint action to take place.

The demarcation line between the three networks is solely analytical in nature. In theory a three-fold dynamic is conceivable: (1) the development of the network itself, (2) the development of EWCs and (3) the development of trade union activity (collective bargaining, sectoral social dialogue). All three strands of development could, under optimal circumstances, stabilise and strengthen each other. Within this framework EWCs would make an important contribution to the formation and stabilisation of a multi-level system of European industrial relations characterised by transnational arenas of industrial relations in which the workplace-based, enterprise-focused level is linked – with mutual advantage – to the meso-level of employment regulation and collective bargaining.

Our research found that although those engaged in EWC work have expressed a need and desire to move in this direction, actual structures are, at best, rudimentary and highly fragmented. There is a large gulf between the normative, deductive and strategic foundations for networks described here and reality. This raises the question as to the probable and desirable paths of development of European industrial relations during a phase of fundamental economic and political restructuring in Europe.

Notes

1   Overall, a fourfold need for the development of EWCs can be noted. i) Quantitatively, at the time of writing, EWCs had been established in around one-third of companies covered by the Directive: the pace of newly-agreed EWCs slowed down markedly after the transposition deadline for the Directive into national legislation, which ended the period of 'voluntary EWCs', on 22 September 1996 (see Chap. 2:1). ii) Qualitatively, many EWCs are still at an early stage of development and have not yet tapped their potential. iii) EWCs embrace only a fraction of companies' geographical scope – at most their European operations. In some EWCs, the requirements of the Directive are exceeded in that representatives from Switzerland and Eastern Europe are included, although this is not the norm. Moreover, global companies raise the issue of worldwide co-operation by trade union and workplace employee representatives: as yet, such co-operation is the exception, not least because of the absence of a political and legal framework to promote and stabilise such a development. iv) Many EWCs do not use the synergies which emerge when they step outside their isolation within the employing company and network with other EWCs and integrate their activity with other trade union fields of activity. This chapter is concerned solely with the latter of these points.

2   The EWC chair at Nestlé was passionate in his advocacy of an efficient organisation of inter-company structures in order to avoid the frustration of increasingly unfocused meetings. The first stages of internationally strategically planned networks can be found in the Netherlands and in the German food industry.

3   Seen in this way, a functioning EWC is itself a network – namely the bringing together of previously independently acting national employee representatives, setting in train an dynamic process of mutual understanding and co-operation.

4   FIET's Geneva office employed 26 people. Although an affiliate of the ETUC, FIET had refused to accord with the ETUC's call to orient itself more strongly to Brussels and create the corresponding political and organisational structures.

5   'Workplace agreements' *(Betriebsvereinbarungen)* are concluded by works councils at various levels in a company. They do not regulate basic pay or the duration of working hours, but may determine how industry-wide provisions on these issues are implemented at company-level, in particular on working time flexibility or performance pay: in addition, they may regulate employee benefits not specified in industry agreements.

6   Project networks could prove counter-productive in the development of individual EWCs were EWC members (in particular from the group's HQ) to have a greater interest in the network than in developing their EWC because they obtain information of more relevance to them via the network and, as a result, neglect their EWC obligations.

5 EWCs in a European Multi-level System of Industrial Relations

Europeanisation of Industrial Relations

In the view of the 'sceptical' mainstream of industrial relations research, three – interrelated – factors stand in the way of the emergence of transnational industrial relations, and in particular of a system of genuinely supranational collective bargaining. The first is the 'European transnational weakness' of the trade unions (rooted in the political, ideological and substantive heterogeneity of union interests). The second is the 'transnational organisational weakness' of the employers (based on the fact that they see no strategic benefit in organising and interacting supra-nationally for the purpose of collective bargaining within the EU framework). And the third is 'the supranational weakness' of the European Union itself as a political entity (Ebbinghaus and Visser, 1994). In particular, corporatist approaches view this lack of a properly functioning statehood, when compared with national states, as telling evidence for the fact that a pattern of industrial relations analogous to the tripartite arrangements found at national level will not be installed at European level in the foreseeable future. Although movement towards statehood might be inherent in the process of European unity, the EU's intrinsic limitations – both as a state and as a democratic polity – serve to block the full realisation of this potential.

> This democratic dilemma of the European order is... symptomatic of an unexpected, long-term and conflictual relationship between the central institutions of the nation state and democratic order on the one hand and a supranational 'emerging statehood' on the other, with unpredictable consequences for the development of democracies in an integrated Europe. By contrast fundamental changes in the political institutions, processes and social structures of the member states are already evident (Bach, 1998, p. 454).

This transitional status also characterises the field of industrial relations. For example, there is as yet no coherent set of instruments for collective employment regulation at European-level and the European system of interest intermediation remains highly fragmented and pluralistic. Measured against the degree of European economic integration, trade union policy on Europe suffers from a marked a 'transnationalisation lag' (Platzer, 1991). Given this, it is not surprising that employers associations will only engage in negotiations with the trade unions at European level under the direct pressure of the imminent adoption of employment related Directives, and then after protracted resistance.

None the less, developments during the 1990s, following the Maastricht treaties, give some grounds for reconsidering and retheorising customary approaches to industrial relations (Platzer, 1998a). Following Maastricht, a tripolar network structure is beginning to emerge within the European-trans national space. In addition to the top level organisations of ETUC, UNICE and CEEP ('compensatory' social dialogue on EU Directives) and occasional, although still infrequent, sectoral social dialogue (as in construction and more recently in shipping and railways), the primary element in this structure is the enterprise level of European Works Councils (EWCs). EWCs currently represent the most dynamic pole within the transnationalisation of industrial relations, are likely to remain so for the foreseeable future, and will constitute a core element in any future European industrial relations. They offer new arenas for transnational information and consultation, and hold out the prospect of co-ordinating enterprise-based relationships between EWCs, trade unions and corporate managements. The EWC typology offered in Chapter 3, especially as it applies to project-oriented and participative EWCs, serves to underline this trend. The respondents in our survey were unambiguous in expressing the need for EWCs to be networked. EWCs will become both a dynamic jumping off point as well as a firm anchor for an emerging European multi-level system of industrial relations, provided the trade unions succeed in utilising and developing the transnational resource which EWCs represent, can network them across companies at sectoral or subsectoral level, and can link this to their own national and European strategies.

As a consequence, the concept of multi-level regulation, which originated in political science (Jachtenfuchs and Kohler-Koch, 1996; Leibfried and Piersson, 1998), might also prove helpful in explaining the development of a cross-border system of industrial relations in Europe. There are a number of indicators to suggest that such a system is gradually developing. Of note is the growing incorporation of European interest associations in the political process at European level, where the Commission is required to consult with employers associations and trade unions whilst preparing draft Directives in the employment field. Such bodies are also represented in countless advisory forums within the EU. The conclusion of the Maastricht Treaty led to the emergence of multi-sectoral dialogue (Falkner, 1998) and also the relaunch of sectoral dialogue (Sörries, 1998) – both preconditions for the regulation of industrial relations at European level. As already noted, sectoral dialogue on temporary work has already taken place in the construction industry, and Directives on parental leave and part time work have been adopted at multi-sectoral level. At the time of writing further Directives on the European Company Statute, temporary agency employment, and information and consultation at national level were under discussion.

Both the trade unions and employers organisations have undertaken a number of organisational steps to adapt to this. These have included a structural reform of the ETUC, which entailed incorporating sectoral-level organisations into the confederation. For the employers' side, special co-ordination structures have been set up within UNICE, such as the European Employers Network to which around sixty European branch associations belong. Both sides have also made adaptations at national level and European issues are becoming increasingly important in the everyday affairs of unions and employer organisations. For example, not only have trade unions established international departments and appointed European specialists but have also created roles for dealing with European issues as they affect all areas of union work. In a more far-reaching step, individual European projects – such as the national EWC project organised by the German metalworkers union IG Metall – have been organised on an interdepartmental basis, a novelty for this trade union. Again at national level the German Confederation of Employers Associations (BDA) has established a 'co-ordination circle' for its main sectoral affiliates which, for their part, are also members of European branch level organisations. These are all institutional innovations induced by the European dimension that have served to create and prepare the basis for a transnationalisation and Europeanisation of industrial relations.

EWCs in the Developing System of European Industrial Relations

Legally secure and firmly institutionalised through the transposition of the EWC Directive into national law, EWCs represent the most dynamic element within this developing and complex network of relationships at the national, transnational and supranational levels of industrial relations. Despite the short period of time for which they have been operating and the difficulties they face, our research shows that EWCs are moving towards constituting a creative core to the process of Europeanising industrial relations. Even during their initial constitutive phase, and in particular in the context of the practical prospects illustrated by the three active EWC types described in Chapter 3, they have been repeatedly forced to confront the problem of operating within a multi-level context both as far as representing their constituencies and taking action is concerned, and of minimising frictional losses and generating synergies between levels. EWCs can only make full use of their structural, institutional, personal and political capacities if they can arrive at efficient solutions to the multi-level problem as presented in the structure of the companies in which they operate. This can be represented at three levels (see diagram).

1)   EWCs' national linkages,

2)   transnational relationships,

3)   European identity.

Three sets of institutional and functional referents can be distinguished for each of these levels: 'EWC internal referents', 'EWC external referents' and 'Fields of activity' (see below). Research into EWCs, and the typology derived from it, as set out in Chapter 3, allow us to identify internal lines of contact and communication and external relationships (networks), and their corresponding main fields of activity. This is depicted diagrammatically in terms of a multi-level system (see diagram on p. 123).

Internal EWC Referents in a Multi-level System

Internal EWC referents at *national level* embrace the provision of information and exchanges of resources between EWC members and national workforce representatives. This connection is particularly important because it creates the link between the traditional national-level role and the new EWC representative role for the individuals who make up the body. Not only do EWCs derive their legitimacy from different sources (in most but not all cases national election and European appointment) but the role brings with it the major problems of time and possibly money. According to our research, workforce representatives in the EWC use a much greater proportion of their time for their national than for their new European tasks (Lecher, 1998b). This can be a major problem during the initial phases of the establishment of EWCs because of the large number of issues to be resolved (language, different national systems of industrial relations, undefined scope of the task). At the same time, any time dedicated to EWC work must be legitimated vis-à-

European Works Councils in the European multi-level system

institutional-functional / spatial-political	EWC Internal referents	EWC External referents (networks)
National linkages	Mutual transfer of resources between EWCs and national systems of employee representation *Fields of activity* Forwarding of information on companies	Contacts to other national EWCs from the same (sub-) sector National structures for trade union EWC support *Fields of activity* Exchange on EWC practice Comparing national indicators relevant to location decisions Exchange of opinions on contents of project
Transnational connections	Mutual support by EWC members *Fields of activity* Building stable information structures within EWCs (in particular between parent company EWC and subsidiaries, and between subsidiaries) Forwarding information on group-level developments and exchange of information on constituent companies and workplaces Construction of a common information platform	Contacts between national EWCs in the same (sub)-sectorT- Transnational contacts between trade union officials responsible for particular undertakings *Fields of activity* Experience sharing on national industrial relations systems – as transnational communication and for evaluation Branch-level compilation of information in the form of services and projects Help in transnational co-ordination of collective bargaining
European identity	Internal EWC balancing of national differences of power and information access Overcoming parent company dominance Internal EWC processes of consensus-building *Fields of activity* Issuing opinions Negotiations with group management (prerequisite: joint work on issues, including setting aims and developing common positions)	Developing common positions and building consensus between various national EWCs from the same (sub)-sector 'Task Force' EWCs in the European industry trade unions *Fields of activity* EWCs conduct their own lobbying and public relations (possibly in agreement with 'related' EWCs) Development of joint negotiating positions on the part of different EWCs – extending to preparation of model agreements Agreements concluded in the network and with trade unions

vis the national representative body that 'delegates' EWC members. During the early stages of an EWC it is difficult to show results which can compare with those achieved at national level. Even when a positive result is obtained it is often difficult to communicate this. The use by EWC members of financial resources provided through national systems of employee representation could also prove problematic: over time it could lead to national dependencies and create hierarchies within the EWC based solely on members' access to national financial resources.

At the level of *transnational relationships* the issue is that of the mutual support provided by EWC members. Research suggests the most prevalent initial arrangement is a radial structure of communication and information provision, at the heart of which is the EWC chair from the country of the parent company with, at best, bilateral contacts to subsidiaries. However, a stable overall EWC structure needs a transnational network of information and communication capable of facilitating direct – and not merely indirect – contact between EWC members.

One important step at the level of European *identity* involves deliberate efforts to limit the dominance of the parent company and establish an internal balance between national differences in information access and power. Parent company dominance can have ambivalent consequences for an EWC. It can pose a problem if an attempt is made to impose industrial relations arrangements and approaches in the parent company on to the EWC. At the same time, it can prove helpful if the strength enjoyed by members from the parent company is used to channel resources to the EWC. This can take place, for example, where group management has agreed improvements in the position of the EWC as a whole with parent company representatives – acting in consultation with members from subsidiaries – on such issues as the scope of information, provision of a formalised consultation procedure and the initiation of projects. One way to deal with the problem of domination by a single national group on the EWC is to establish a joint steering committee with representatives from the parent company and subsidiaries, with a conscious attempt to avoid domination by any one grouping. At supranational level the issue is to attain a balance within the EWC in which no one group or individual member becomes dominant or gains maximum advantage but in which the combined interests of the body as a whole are optimised.

External EWC Referents in the Multi-level System

We now consider the EWC's external relationships. As far as the level of *national* linkages is concerned – either of the body as a whole or individual members – contacts to other national EWCs in the same sector or sub-sector constitute one useful strand. Examples of such networks (cf. Chapter 4) already exist in the Netherlands and initiatives are in train in Germany. There are also some instances of individual EWCs being supported by dedicated trade union officials in the home country of the parent company. Our study points to a strategic need to extend national EWC networks and root them in appropriate trade union support structures.

At the level of *transnational* relationships, contacts between different national EWCs in the same sector or sub-sector are also conceivable. However, such contacts are much more difficult to establish, stabilise and develop when compared with national-level links. Not only is there the common fact of economic competition between companies, but the compounding effect of the basic difficulties encountered in all EWCs (language, time, money, industrial relations infrastructure). Parallel transnational contacts between the respective responsible union officials, whose task would be to co-ordinate such EWC networks, could pay a positive role in providing support.

At *European* level, the key component in EWCs' external relationships consists of processes to secure agreement and co-ordinate positions between national EWCs in the same sector or sub-sector. These would initially take the form of informal contacts on an issue-by-issue basis that could, in the course of time, be consolidated into firmer networks. This would allow EWCs to overcome their corporate isolation. In addition, by giving them access to more information – and possibly in the longer term to mutual solidarity – it would endow them with greater competence and certainty both when acting alone and in conjunction with others. It would fall to trade unions to accept – and take seriously – the positions adopted by EWCs and, in an advisory activity, prepare for a role in which they would support and co-ordinate such activities.

EWC Fields of Activity in the Multi-level System

As the diagram ('EWC Fields of Activity in the Multi-level System', p. 123) shows, EWCs' institutional-functional referents at each spatial level are allotted to fields of activity which can be differentiated – both according to the logic of the matrix and also in terms of current and prospective practice – into internal and network referents. In order to simplify the presentation we dispense with this distinction below: that is, fields of activity are dealt with as integrated complexes of activities at specific levels. This also corresponds with the perception of how EWCs function in practice.

For example, at *national* level information about companies is passed from EWCs to national representative institutions; conversely, national-level information of importance for the work of EWCs will be collected locally and made available to the European body – with EWCs acting as a catalyst. Of particular importance at this level is information on questions of where operations are located, especially if group management is planning or implementing an international restructuring project. Experience suggests that it is almost impossible to exclude this potentially very troubling and demanding issue, which affects all levels in a developed EWC, from the scope of EWC activity. Indeed, it is precisely in such situations that employees are most in need of help from their EWC. Rather it seems more sensible, and more in line with the expectations placed on EWCs, to tackle the issue head on and make it a priority, specifically as far as the information exchanged between EWC and national structures of representation is concerned. That this can lead on to EWCs being able to exercise some influence on agreements is evidenced by some initial examples, such as Bull and Schmalbach-Lubeca (Lecher et.al., 1999). Such cases also show that the absence of information and reliable forecasting which can characterise international restructuring also force managements themselves to act under conditions of great uncertainty. Research into mergers and acquisitions indicates that around half of all mergers and as much as two-thirds of large-scale mergers fail.

In addition, analysis of and information on national management behaviour and national industrial relations systems – themselves already engaged in the transition to a transnational level of relationships – can boost the internal cohesion of the EWC, overcome prejudice and allow a more realistic and accurate assessment of national patterns of industrial relations, which may be very different from the level of central corporate management. Possible steps towards a national EWC network might include sharing experience on organisational and technical aspects of EWC work, exchanging information and opinions on projects, and building a joint approach to external relations.

The activities of service and project-oriented EWCs would need to be located at the *transnational* level, where information can be systematically collected and co-ordinated and where EWC projects, or projects carried out jointly with management, could be initiated, implemented, evaluated, and fed through into more long-term practice. Suitable issues might include, initially, responses to EU Directives impacting directly on conditions of employment (such as environmental audits, health and safety matters, implementing parental leave). They could also embrace independent projects conducted by the EWC on matters such as equality of opportunity, continuing training, data protection and personnel information systems. Independent projects not only raise the standing of the EWC vis-à-vis management but could also stimulate multi-industry and in particular sectoral dialogue at EU-level. Active EWCs could also stimulate better linkages between the EWC-level and European social dialogue. For example, they would be well-placed to play an important role in collecting and compiling data on issues relevant to collective bargaining and to make these available to trade unions engaged in the transnational co-ordination of sectoral bargaining (Schulten, 1998).

At the most developed level of *European identity,* EWCs might be able to work out common internal positions, including outlining possible activities, for presentation to group management. This could take place at enterprise level, but is also conceiveable in a form which brings together EWCs from several groups, culminating in distinctive EWC lobbying and external relations. For example, EWCs could engage in negotiations with the aim of concluding 'pilot' or 'pattern' agreements with the support of trade unions. The range of activities undertaken by supra-nationally operating EWCs would undoubtedly be troubling for the trade unions as it would directly impinge on their own role and legitimacy as employee representatives. This applies with particular force for trade unions that have customarily exercised a leadership role in workplace representation, and also for dualistic systems of industrial relations. However, building EWCs that are effective vis-à-vis management and competent partners at the increasingly important European level means that there is no alternative to developing effective co-ordination and a division of labour between EWCs and trade unions. The fact that national trade unions have deep and understandable anxieties about the impact of this on their 'core competence' of collective bargaining has, as yet, made it difficult for them to tackle the question of the Europeanisation of collective bargaining, despite the intensification of Europeanisation triggered by Economic and Monetary Union (Lecher, 1999).

EWCs and Collective Bargaining

The Social Agreement attached to the Maastricht Treaty, now incorporated into the Social Chapter of the Amsterdam Treaty, provides for an extension of the basis for EU activity in the social and employment field and strengthens the role of the European social partners – although expressly excluding freedom of association and industrial action from the range of issues which can be regulated at EU-level. At the same time there is a strong feeling among some decision-makers that policies to promote employment under EMU require a sustained and balanced mix of monetary, fiscal and wage policy. The development of a European system of industrial relations at sectoral level, which in most EU member states remains the main level for collective bargaining, cannot, however, be induced by decree. In turn, as long as there is no actual practice which can drive forward and shape the development of law, there will be no European right of association, and no legal regulation of industrial action and collective agreements. Progress on the legal front presupposes large-scale transnationally co-ordinated European bargaining. And – as historical experience has shown – this will initially and primarily be based on the autonomous capacity of the European trade unions. Despite the refusal of employers' associations to accept a European dimension to collective bargaining, some steps in this direction are possible (Traxler, 1996). European comparisons already play a role in national collective bargaining and this may well intensify under EMU. For example, some collective agreements in Belgium and the Netherlands make express references to agreed provisions in adjoining regions in other countries (notably, in this case, North-Rhine Westphalia).

EWCs could play an important role in this new field of transnationally co-ordinated European bargaining. At the level of transnational relations they could collect data on relevant issues, including the core fields of pay and working time in those countries to which they have access as EWCs, and make this information available to trade unions. In addition, EWC projects could be established to build an enterprise-based, trade union oriented approach to collective bargaining in conjunction with national relevant trade unions. Through co-operation with trade union transnational bodies for information and co-ordination, this could provide the germ of a system of European collective bargaining. Although such a prospect would have ambivalent implications for union-based employee representation 'why should European collective bargaining not have at its core, for example, cross-border enterprise-level collective agreements on issues such as work organisation, health and safety and outsourcing?' (Eller-Braatz and Klebe, 1998, p. 450). It would be possible, initially at least, for 'soft' issues such as health and safety or training to be negotiated between EWCs and group managements, with the 'harder' traditional issues, such as pay and working time, reserved for trade unions and their transnationally co-ordinated sectoral collective bargaining. Such an approach is not only a threat, therefore, but also an opportunity to Europeanise collective bargaining.

Beginning with initiatives in transnational co-ordination, collective bargaining could progressively free itself from its – now economically overly restrictive – national casing and open itself to greater Europeanisation. Some experience has already been gathered with building transnational information networks. EWCs offer a means of broadening and developing these initiatives. Trade unions could choose on which issues and on what timescale the process should proceed. By campaigning on issues which point towards greater Europeanisation, both at national and European sectoral level, they could also gain a strategic advantage over employers' organisations in what is for them a critical field. EWCs would also offer a means of stabilising collective bargaining on a transnational basis under the conditions set by EMU. Finally, EWCs could offer benefits in the field of workplace codetermination, should any future revision of the EWC Directive yield a broader definition of information and a more specific requirement on consultation.

EWCs and Sectoral Social Dialogue

The emergence and development of social dialogue has passed through three stages, viewed in terms of the history of European integration. The weakly developed 'tri-partism' of the 1970s and 1980s was followed, after 1986, by the ('old') social dialogue promoted by Commission president Jaques Delors – the 'Val Duchesse' process – as means of developing a 'social dimension' to the internal market. This led on to an extended form of social dialogue based on the joint accord between the European social partner organisations and was anchored as the 'new' social dialogue in the Maastricht Treaty.

This guaranteed the social partners formalised scope for consultation in all social policy legislative initiatives put forward by the Commission and the option of 'contractual relations, including the conclusion of agreements' (Article 4, Paragraph 1 of the Social Agreement).

This constitutional innovation has to be seen in the context of the Maastricht 'Grand Bargain', which extended the EU's social and employment powers and changed decision making procedures in parallel with measures to inaugurate economic and monetary union, a phase only concluded with the Amsterdam Treaty which ended the British opt out. The Maastricht Treaty – in the spirit of subsidiarity – also gave the semi-autonomous conclusion of agreements by the social partners priority over statutory regulation. This applied both at the European peak-level organisations of trade unions and employers as well as the meso-level of sectoral organisations.

Whether this has served to establish a 'corporatist policy regime' (Falkner, 1998) in the field of European social and employment policy and the extent to which it has prepared the ground for a system of European collective bargaining with a supranational dimension have been judged very differently in the literature and still elude any truly satisfactory theoretical treatment (Keller and Sörries, 1998; Platzer, 1998a, 1998b; Schulten, 1998). As shown at a number of points in this study (in particular, Chapter 2) the development of sectoral dialogue is only really underway in a small number of branches, with substantial variation in the terms of the consultative arrangements adopted, the issues on which consultation takes place, and the results. As yet it remains less dynamic than multi-industry social dialogue. None the less, since the mid-1990s there has been an intensification of interaction between European trade unions and employers associations in an expanding number of sectors. Promoted by the European Commission in its role as 'process manager', this has meant that more framework accords are now possible.

In addition to the sectoral accords which have already been concluded – in agriculture and merchant shipping – agreements were also imminent on working time flexibility and health and safety in banking and agriculture at the time this study was concluded.

Given the very diverse pattern of sectoral social dialogue, what relationship prevails, and could prevail, between the development and networking of EWCs and the emergence of a system of European industrial relations at branch and sub-sectoral level? Assuming that the significance of those agreements already concluded is more procedural than substantive, that is it consists primarily in the fact that new procedural options have been developed, refined and custom and practice established, and given the quantitative and qualitative stage of development of EWCs (Chapter 3) it is hardly surprising that genuine interaction between these two levels of activity remains of marginal importance. At the same time – as our research has shown – the need for and possibility of strengthening the links between these two dimensions and placing them on a more systematic basis has been recognised and argued for by both workplace and trade union actors.

Even if these perceptions contain a voluntaristic element, it is possible to imagine scenarios in which paths towards Europeanisation emerge based on a mutual exchange of information or political impulses between EWC level and sectoral social dialogue. Each level of actor and of activity would acquire a specific role both in agenda setting and in negotiating and implementing agreements.

Bottom up impulses from workplace to sectoral level could be generated through situations in which EWCs have the capacities denoted above as 'project networks', given a need for regulation at inter-company and branch-level which is sufficiently evident and backed up by appropriate information to allow priorities and agenda setting for sectoral social dialogue to take place and enjoy legitimacy. Given the unwillingness, or only occasional willingness, of many sectoral employers associations to negotiate – either because of their organisational structure or an assessment of their interests – such an impulse would not be sufficient in itself to initiate sectoral negotiations. Only through the pressure which could be generated by the sort of EWC grouping described here as an 'action network' would it be possible – given strategic mediation by the sectoral European industry federations – to achieve agreed regulations within the framework of sectoral social dialogue.

Implementing European social partner agreements is fraught with legal and political problems. Those agreements concluded so far have been transposed into legislation via a decision of the Council of Ministers. This will have been associated with top down effects as far as the issues dealt with by EWCs as well their practical tasks are concerned.

The more that EU social and employment regulation shifts from the principle of 'hard' substantive regulation via law towards 'soft' optional and procedural 'negotiated legislation' determined by the European social partners, the more significant will be the issue of how European framework regulations are transposed to and implemented at lower levels. Within such a perspective, in which implementation acquires a specific status within the overall policy cycle, EWCs would be accorded a 'naturally' significant role. Framework agreements which have already been negotiated offer scope for concretisation and transposition at workplace level, and hence suggest an authentic field of activity for EWCs.

EWC Prospects in a Multi-level System of European Industrial Relations

As far as the activity and perspectives of an EWC is concerned, the multi-level system does not consist of a set of separate and exclusive tiers but as an overarching framework. The difficulty lies in the fact that EWCs must operate simultaneously at national level, at transnational level, and, in terms of developing an identity, in particular at the specifically European level. The latter requires stable national links and the development of a well-functioning network of transnational relations, as the example of collective bargaining shows. This also applies for a further current and potential core area of EWC activity. In the diagram (see p. 123) the issue of 'location decisions' is only placed in the top right-hand box which matches 'national linkages' and 'EWC external referents'. However this is intended to imply simply that even at this lowest level of EWC activity the collection of data on location issues makes good sense. At the level of transnational relations it would be possible to evaluate information on local operations in terms of threats to any particular site, whilst at European level – on the assumption that an EWC has acquired the capacity to take action and wishes to engage in this field – the EWC would need to develop positions which could be put forward in the context of negotiations with central management. Trade union experts would need to be drawn in especially for the second and third step.

As far as the process of their constitution is concerned, EWCs can be understood as a succession of steps ranging from national linkages to the emergence of a European identity. At the same time, they are constantly called on to link the various levels and arenas in which they operate – either actually or prospectively. The networks which operate for and around EWCs can prove useful in facilitating this complex task by serving as stabilisers for EWCs that are isolated, and often overburdened, within the framework of their employing organisations. EWCs are reliant on specific support services in each of their fields of activity. Networks can deliver these services and render them more effective, becoming optimised when they see themselves as part of a European multi-level system. This will also serve to strengthen national domestic structures, those initial transnational bridgeheads which have been established and the, as yet, minimally developed supra-national EU trade union structures and give all of these greater European capability and significance.

6 Prospects: EWCs – Between Forum, Actor and Network

The manner in which EWCs have tackled the problems encountered in constituting themselves, against the background of the rich experience of the practice of workplace employee representation at national level, is adding momentum to a process which extends beyond the provisions of EWC Directive and EWC agreements.[1] Although the law limits employee participation to information and consultation, the practice of EWCs 'suggests that the processes for establishing new procedures and institutions set in train by these agreements will not necessarily stop at the boundaries imposed by these definitions and the law' (Höland, 1997, p. 60). This applies, for example, to the Directive's restrictive understanding of consultation, which it defines as 'the exchange of views and establishment of dialogue between employees' representatives and central management or any other more appropriate level of management'. It also applies to the capacity of EWCs to conclude agreements: in many instance they have already acquired experience of bargaining with corporate management through 'negotiating in their own cause' to improve existing voluntary agreements. None the less, the development of EWCs remains very varied (see Chapter 3).

EWCs are frequently dealt with by corporate managements simply as an information forum and not as an industrial relations actor. Consultation is limited to an exchange of views. Many EWC representatives are also critical of how managements deal with the provision of information, and in particular the failure to make information available at the proper time, in writing and in sufficient detail. At the same time, the lack of access to external experts creates problems in dealing with and evaluating complex financial, strategic, technical and organisational information. Despite this, many EWC representatives feel that EWCs must focus on questions of corporate strategy or – in a slightly weaker variant – on the personnel consequences of corporate strategy. Such a strategic perspective tends to be absent where the European conditions for national action are accorded only a low priority. Even in these cases, however, there is an awareness that EWCs will grow in importance, not least because of Economic and Monetary Union, which will accelerate the emergence of a European labour market at enterprise level.

133

The question of information and consultation on strategic corporate decisions, and on restructuring and rationalisation measures with a cross-border dimension, will remain a central concern for EWCs given continuing international mergers and acquisitions. However, an EWC will only be able to put forward its own proposals if it has been informed at the planning stage and has the capacity to assess the proposed measures in terms of their business rationality and social impact, based on previous experience and available skills. As yet, only a few EWCs have had experience with consultation. In the main, group managements have determined the scope and intensity of the consultation process. At the same time, managements are also often confronted with questions and demands from EWCs which flow from their decisions – such as workforce reductions in subsidiaries. For the most part EWCs are dissatisfied with practice so far, arguing that EWCs must be in a position to decide the issues on which information and consultation will take place and, in the longer term, possibly be negotiated on. Although most managements reject formal negotiations with EWCs there are some precedents (such as Danone) which will make it more difficult for employers to continue to justify this stance, especially in the light of agreements concluded at (multi-) sectoral level.

Informal negotiations between EWCs and group managements have also taken place in only a few instances, although negotiations are widely viewed as a likely option for the future. In addition to 'soft' qualitative issues, negotiations are also likely to deal with some of the classical substantive negotiating questions. Collective bargaining on consensual themes was seen as a second order issue by the EWC members interviewed for this study, albeit one which often serves as a means of initiating the negotiating process and building trust with group management. Although EWCs are formally confined to information and consultation, the logic of their role as representatives could be seen as pushing out beyond this: for example, several EWCs have negotiated with group managements to adapt voluntary agreements to the standards set by the Directive. The trend towards decentralising industrial relations to enterprise and workplace level together with the growth of cross-border trade union structures suggest that, provided there is union support, the negotiating capacity of EWCs is likely to grow.

In this connection, projects defined and pursued jointly with group management might constitute a link between information and consultation, on the one hand, and negotiation on the other. Projects demarcate a terrain on which both sides have an interest in collaboration. Where successful, joint projects could help stabilise the joint committee since the added-value of EWCs will also accrue to management. In the most favourable scenario, joint projects could also influence management decisions more generally, and would therefore be consistent with the aim of seeking to influence corporate decisions. Confining the activity of joint committees to information disclosure and the implementation of projects would, however, limit their terrain to a sphere below what might be designated the European level of employee interest representation proper. This level is only fully constituted when EWCs develop a way of working in the fields of information, consultation, and negotiation which offers the prospect of influencing group-level business, financial and personnel decisions. The possibility of negotiations between EWCs and group managements raises the question as to how national and European trade unions can secure access to information and involvement, and how different bargaining arenas can be integrated.

The internal constitution of EWCs, in the sense of the establishment of their own operational and organisational structures and means of communication, remains – as our case studies show – often incomplete. Building an internal information system remains the central task. The majority of EWC members interviewed for this study said they did not want to restrict their activity to a single annual meeting of the joint session with management but were keen to develop forums which can sustain contact and activity. This would entail intensifying communications between meetings and creating structures for activity and organisation. Although pre-meetings and to a lesser extent follow-up meetings, together with a steering committee of employee representatives, in many cases represent a standard agreed with group management, an annual meeting of the entire EWC together with a few meetings of the steering committee do not represent a working structure. In particular, select committees have not usually become the organising centre of the EWC, responsible for maintaining the dynamic of activity and setting strategy. EWC representatives on the select committee are often preoccupied with problems brought to them by representatives from subsidiary companies, such as restructuring and redundancies. Finally, more intense communication within the EWC is frequently handicapped by socio-cultural obstacles (language, lack of knowledge of other countries industrial relations and regulatory systems, low trust, uncertainty about the value and function of the EWC) and structural barriers (lack of appropriate communication infrastructure, lack of procedural rules for information exchange, lack of an organising centre for the EWC, political competition between trade unions, lack of continuity in staffing of EWC, size and heterogeneity of the forum and lack of sub-committees).

One of the most fundamental problems is that of the relationship between trade unions and EWCs. How this tricky relationship is organised will be of great significance for how the Europeanisation of industrial relations will develop.

In addition to the broader and unresolved issue of trade union strategies for Europe, the creation of effective and extensive links between EWCs and trade unions is primarily a problem of resources. EWC representatives understand this and are often modest in the demands they place on trade unions. Our study also shows that EWCs desire greater autonomy from trade unions, but do not wish to de-link the two entirely. German employee representatives in particular regard EWC activity as essentially their responsibility, with trade unions offering more of an advisory than a leadership role: they expect the unions to grant them the appropriate freedom of action to pursue this. In their view, co-ordinating national employee representatives can be carried out by the EWC itself. EWCs are nonetheless keen to maintain a dialogue with the trade unions: they are aware of their limitations and expect more from trade unions than a mere servicing role. For example, they need regular information on developments at European level, such as new legislation, to enable them to build on European regulations. Trade unions should also work with EWCs when putting forward demands at European level to enable them to be pursued jointly. EWC representatives consider that any extension of employee rights at European level can only occur through pressure from trade unions and works councils, for which the national level interaction between workplace and collectively agreed provisions offers a precedent, at least in most EU Member States. In some cases, having provisions already installed at workplace level is a precondition for winning the same in industry-level collective agreements.

As far as ongoing EWC work is concerned, employee representatives see the unions as exercising more of a co-ordinating than a leadership role in the future – for example by acting as an intermediary between different levels and arenas of policy, as well as facilitating the exchange of information and co-operation between EWCs. Unions are also seen as responsible for collating the experience and information acquired by EWCs and offering an overall strategic direction. To do this they need to be integrated into EWCs' information networks: as yet, however, this remains only rudimentary.

In addition to their relationships to trade unions, EWCs' links with national representation arrangements represent a second problem area. As yet few national employee representatives are convinced that EWCs are important for their work. In addition to the lack of practical experience seen in 'young' EWCs, and the associated lack of clear evidence that European activity can add value to employee representation, this perception is also attributable to inadequate trade union engagement in explaining the role of EWCs.

These three elements can also be seen at work in the third problem area – low or entirely absent employee interest in the activity of EWCs. EWCs often have a very low profile at the immediate workplace: their very existence and work often go unmentioned even at formal events such as the regular staff meetings held under German works councils legislation, a central focus of communication between elected representatives and workforces. The relationship between workforces and EWCs in the German case could be described as 'second order delegation'. Employee interest often ends with elections to workplace-level institutions. Although this institutional-functional understanding of interest representation stands in blatant contradiction to the observation that 'participation and information have become central demands of all employee groups' (Marstedt et.al., 1993, p. 93), such a demand is not automatically translated into an identification with workplace institutions for employee representation, which are often hostile to or sceptical about broader vehicles for employee participation. On the other hand, EWC representatives are usually aware of the importance of mediating between the local and the European level. The upward transmission of information is seen as a necessary part of developing an EWC's own information system. EWC members can only forward information to the EWC if they have already acquired it locally. A downward flow of information is intended to help gain acceptance of the forum at workplace level, but is also needed in its own right to implement EWC policies. This applies especially where agreements between EWC and group management need to be fleshed out locally.

Against this background of existing practice, an exchange of experience between EWCs in different companies could help structure what is still largely an unexplored terrain in the field of employee representation and develop standards for employee representation at European level. This applies both for the internal organisation of communication and working procedures as well as to issues for consideration by the joint committee with management. It also applies to the experiences which EWC representatives have had with trade unions and the local workplace level. However, this would require EWC representatives to take a more political view of their activity since they would need to detach their experiences and the problems encountered in their work from their immediate corporate context. As a consequence, it would be important to choose issues and problems of more general significance and which are likely to confront other EWCs in the short or longer run. This might begin with areas already regulated at European level – such as health and safety, environmental protection, collective dismissals, equality of opportunity, and parental leave. A further category might include issues which are the subject of social dialogue, such as employment and training. A third area could embrace problems experienced by most EWCs for which some common standards might be appropriate: for example, mergers and acquisitions, restructuring, closures and transfers of operations. A further group could consist of issues on which there is overlap with collective bargaining or national legislation, such as pay and working time. And a final category would consist of issues that have traditionally been dealt with at company level, such as workplace benefits.

Joint consideration by EWCs of the situation and development of individual branches, of corporate strategies and the position of different companies within the branch is a further area which could be dealt with within such a framework. This could lead to a more realistic and informed judgement of corporate strategies, enabling EWCs to be more pro-active when facing corporate restructuring. Exchanging information about companies (and forwarding it to trade unions) is seen as a delicate matter because of the constraints of confidentiality. An open exchange of information is also limited by fears that revealing information to third parties could damage one's own employer. In this respect, EWCs are in the same position as employee representatives at national level. National problems are also similar: cuts in workplace benefits, workforce reductions, outsourcing and demergers, longer working hours, and more performance-based pay in relation to basic pay. One task which EWCs and European structures could fulfil would, therefore, be to maintain those standards which have already been reached. This goes hand in hand with the desire to use national standards for the group as a whole.

All these problems and prospects for the development of EWCs serve to re-emphasise the importance of networking, as set out in Chapter 4.

Networking EWCs could prove useful in three respects.

- Firstly, sharing best practice and possibly combining tasks – such as analysing individual branches – could have a direct positive impact on EWC activity.
- Secondly, co-ordinating trade union support for EWCs at branch level could help alleviate the resource problem experienced by trade unions in this area.
- And thirdly, networking EWCs would enable possible areas for negotiation at sectoral level to be explored, opening up a pathway to sectoral negotiations within the context of social dialogue.

At the same time, networking EWCs at European sectoral level could respond to the diverse interests of EWC representatives and take into account the differing levels of development of EWCs. It would also be able to connect with the diverse experiences and structures of networking at national level. By transferring experience, knowledge and information networking could strengthen EWC activity and spread good practice. And by helping EWCs to arrive at and agree common positions, networks could also assume the role of actor in their own right. To do so, they would need to initiate an intensification of sectoral dialogue and raise their own concerns with the EU's political institutions. A network could co-ordinate the strategies of participating EWCs, facilitate agreement, and generally leverage their effectiveness.

Finally, a network could also support the co-ordination of national collective bargaining by compiling information on terms and conditions of employment and making this available to the trade unions, thus linking the European level of employee representation with the trade union co-ordination of collective bargaining. Should the trade unions succeed in establishing close and stable networks with EWCs, both at national and European level, model enterprise-level agreements could provide patterns for branch-level negotiations to follow. As a consequence, EWC networks would need to be complemented by trade union networks at European level. This would relate to officials entrusted with support functions for particular companies or EWCs. Such a network could constitute an important bridge between workplace representation and trade unions, and help integrate the national and European levels. Furthermore, a network of experts would have to be created to deal with specific EWC problems (such as employment law) which could provide prompt advice to EWCs and trade unions when needed.

These possible scenarios for networking are based on existing initiatives. Although for the most part they remain fragmented, there are a number of nodes from which networks might grow. But even if the perception of problem issues and ideas of how these might be tackled suggest a need for networks, and the likelihood of their development, whether the necessary linkages will become a reality remains an open question. Only future developments will reveal whether enterprise-based and sectorally-based industrial relations at European level will develop in a complementary process of evolution which can provide the stability and dynamism needed to establish a dualistic pattern of industrial relations at European level – a pattern for which networks would provide one, albeit not a sufficient, precondition.

The result of this study, and the consequent prospects for the future, can be summarised as follows. Since the early-1990s, and subject to the profound changes in the economic and political context of European integration, significant processes of Europeanisation have begun in the sphere of industrial relations. At the same time, studies of the forms and dynamics of the development of EWCs, together with developments in the sphere of employment and social policy and collective bargaining at the European branch- and macro-level, also reveal the diversity and asynchronicity of this process. None the less, the emergence of transnational arenas and cross-border, supra-national structures of relationships between the social partners, means that the contours of a developing multi-level system of industrial relations are becoming visible. This structural framework and process of development might – but do not have to – lead to the emergence of supra-national levels of regulation in the form of a genuinely European regime of industrial relations. Rather, it suggests in the first instance qualitative changes in the interdependencies and interactions along both a horizontal, cross-border, axis and a vertical axis, embracing the national and the European level in the each of the micro-, macro- and meso-spheres of industrial relations. There remains an enormous need for further empirical and theoretical clarification in this area, requiring more research both in processes of European integration as well as comparative industrial relations. The research set out and analysed in this study will hopefully serve as one building block in such an undertaking.

Note

1   Unless otherwise indicated, the statements and conclusions relate to the research set out above in the food, insurance and banking sectors. In addition, some points may also be derived from the previous study on the metalworking and chemical industries (Lecher, Nagel, Platzer, et.al., 1999).

Bibliography

Armingeon, K. (1994), *Staat und Arbeitsbeziehungen. Ein internationaler Vergleich*, Opladen.

Bach, M. (1998), 'Die Europäische Union zwischen Pseudo-Staatlichkeit und Mehrheitsentscheidung', *Soziologische Revue* 4, pp. 447-454.

Buda, D. (1998), 'On course for European labour relations? The prospects for the Social Dialogue in the European Union', in Lecher, W. and Platzer, H.-W, (eds), *European Union - European Industrial Relations*, London, pp. 21-46.

Busch, K. (1994), *Europäische Integration und Tarifpolitik. Lohnpolitische Konsequenzen der Wirtschafts- und Währungsunion*, Cologne.

Carley, M. and Hall, M. (1996), 'Comparative Analysis of Agreements' in, Bonneton, P., Carley, M., Hall, M., Krieger, H., *Review of Current Agreements on Information and Consultation in European Multinationals*, Luxembourg, pp. 13-40.

Däubler, W. (1997), 'Entwicklung und Perspektiven des europäischen Arbeitsrechts', in Platzer, H.-W. (ed.), *Sozialstaatliche Entwicklungen in Europa und die Sozialpolitik der EU*, Baden-Baden, pp.101-116.

Danis, J.-J. and Hoffmann, R. (1995), 'From the Vredeling Directive to the European Works Council Directive – some historical remarks', *Transfer*, vol. 2, pp. 180-187.

Deppe, J., Hoffmann, R., Stützel, W. (eds.) (1997), *Europäische Betriebsräte. Wege in ein soziales Europa*, Frankfurt am Main.

Ebbinghaus, B. and Visser, J. (1994), 'Barrieren und Wege "grenzenloser Solidarität": Gewerkschaften und europäische Integration', in: W. Streeck (ed.), *Staat und Verbände*, PVS Sonderheft 25/1994, Opladen, pp. 223-255.

Eller-Braatz, E. and Klebe, T. (1998), 'Benchmarking in der Automobilindustrie – Folgen für Betriebs- und Tarifpolitik am Beispiel von General Motors Europe', *WSI-Mitteilungen*, 7/1998.

European Commission (1995), *European Social Dialogue Status Report 1995*, Luxembourg.

European Commission (1998), *European Social Dialogue Status Report 1997*, Luxembourg.

141

Falkner, G. (1998), *EU Social Policy in the 1990s. Towards a corporatist policy community*, London/New York.

Falkner, G. (1996), 'European Works Councils and the Maastricht Social Agreement: Towards a new policy style?', *Journal of European Public Policy*, vol. 6, pp.192- 208.

Habermas, J. (1998) *Die postnationale Konstellation. Politische Essays*, Frankfurt am Main.

Höland, A. (1997*)*, *Mitbestimmung und Europa – Expertise im Rahmen des Projektvorhabens 'Mitbestimmung und neue Unternehmenskulturen – Bilanz und Perspektiven'*, Gütersloh.

Höland, A. (1998), 'Rechtfertigungsdruck', *Die Mitbestimmung* 6/1998, p. 67.

Hoffmann, R. (1996), 'Europäisierung als Modernisierung', in Mückenberger, U., Schmidt, E., Zoll, R. (eds), *Die Modernisierung der Gewerkschaften in Europa*, Münster, pp. 292-344.

Hornung-Draus, R. (1998), 'The Union of Industry and Employers associations in Europe – UNICE', in Lecher, W. and Platzer, H.-W. (eds.), *European Union – European Industrial Relations?*, London, pp. 194-203.

Jachtenfuchs, M. and Kohler-Koch, B. (eds) (1996), 'Europäische Integration – Regieren im dynamischen Mehrebenensystem', in Jachtenfuchs, M. and Kohler-Koch, B. (eds), *Europäische Integration*, Opladen.

Keller, B. (1996), 'Nach der Verabschiedung der Richtlinie zu EBRen – Von enttäuschten Erwartungen, unerfüllbaren Hoffnungen und realistischen Perspektiven', *WSI-Mitteilungen*, 8, pp. 470-482.

Keller, B. and Sörries, B. (1998), 'The new social dialogue: procedural structuring, first results and perspectives', *Industrial Relations Journal. European Annual Review 1997*, Oxford, pp. 77-98.

Krieger, H. and Bonneton, P. (1995), 'Analysis of existing voluntary agreements on information and consultation in European multinationals', *Transfer* 2, pp. 188-206.

Lecher, W. (1998a), 'Auf dem Weg zu europäischen Arbeitsbeziehungen? Das Beispiel der Euro-Betriebsräte', *WSI-Mitteilungen*, 4, pp. 258-263.

Lecher, W. (1998b), 'Resources of the European Works Council – Empirical Knowledge and Prospects', in: Hoffmann, R., Jacobi, O., Keller, B., Weiss, M. (eds), *The German Model of Industrial Relations between Adaptation and Erosion*, Hans Böckler Stiftung, Graue Reihe 145, pp. 123-134.

Lecher, W. (1998c), 'Ressourcen des Europäischen Betriebsrats', *WSI-Mitteilungen*, 10, pp. 691-98.

Lecher, W., Nagel, B., Platzer, H.-W., Fulton, L., Jaich, R., Rehfeldt, U., Rüb, S., Telljohann, V., Weiner, K.-P. (1999), *The Establishment of European Works Councils*, Aldershot.

Lecher, W. and Platzer H.-W. (1998), *European Union – European Industrial Relations?*, London.

Lecher, W., and Platzer H.-W., (1996), 'Europäische Betriebsräte. Fundament und Instrument europäischer Arbeitsbeziehungen?', *WSI-Mitteilungen*, 8, pp. 503-512.

Leibfried, S. and Piersson, P. (ed.) (1998), *Standort Europa. Europäische Sozialpolitik zwischen Nationalstaat und Europäischer Integration*, Frankfurt am Main.

Marginson, P., Gilman, M., Jacobi, O., Krieger, H. (1998), 'Negotiating European Works Councils. An Analysis of Agreements under Article 13', Report prepared for the European Foundation for the Improvement of Living and Working Conditions and the European Commission.

Marginson, P. and Sisson, K. (1996), 'European Works Councils – Opening the Door to European Bargaining?', *Industrielle Beziehungen*, vol 3, no. 3, pp. 229-236.

Martin, A. (1996), 'European institutions and the Europeanisation of trade unions: Support or seduction', Discussion and Working Paper of the European Trade Union Institute, Brussels.

Marstedt, G., Last, R., Wahl, W.-B. and Müller, R. (1993), *Gesundheit und Lebensqualität*, Bremen.

Nagel, B., Riess, B., Rüb, S., Beschorner, A., (1996), *Information und Mitbestimmung im internationalen Konzern*, Baden-Baden.

Platzer, H.-W. (1991), *Gewerkschaftspolitik ohne Grenzen? Die transnationale Zusammenarbeit der Gewerkschaften im Europa der 90er Jahre*, Bonn.

Platzer, H.-W. (1998a), Industrial relations and European Integration. Patterns, Dynamics and Limits of Transnationalisation, in: Lecher, W. and Platzer, H.-W. (eds), *European Union – European Industrial Relations?*, London, pp. 81-120.

Platzer, H.-W. (1998b), 'Arbeitsbeziehungen in der transnationalen Ökonomie und Mehrebenenpolitik der EU. Wandel nationaler Systeme und Europäisierungsprozesse', in Schmid J. and Niketta, R., *Wohlfahrtsstaat. Krise und Reform im Vergleich*. Marburg.

Platzer, H.-W. and Weiner, K.-P. (1998), 'Europäische Betriebsräte - eine Konstitutionsanalyse. Zur Genese und Dynamik transnationaler Arbeitsbeziehungen', *Industrielle Beziehungen*, vol. 5, no. 4, 1998, pp. 388-412.

Rademacher, U. (1996), *Der Europäische Betriebsrat. Die Richtlinie 94/45/ EG des Rates vom 22.9.1994 und ihre Umsetzung in nationales Recht,* Baden-Baden.

Rehfeldt, U. (1998), 'European Works Councils: An assessment of French initiatives' in, Lecher, W. and Platzer, H.-W. (eds), *European Union – European Industrial Relations?,* London, pp. 207-222.

Rehfeldt, U. (1998), 'Der Renault-Vilvoorde-Konflikt und seine Bedeutung für die europäische Gewerkschaftspolitik', *WSI-Mitteilungen,* 7/1998, pp. 450ff.

Rhodes, M. (1997), 'Globalisation, Labour Markets and Welfare States: A Future of "Competitive Corporatism"?', Working Paper of the Robert Schumann Centre, European University Institute, Florence, No. 36.

Schirm, S. (1997), 'Transnationale Globalisierung und regionale Kooperation', *Zeitschrift für internationale Beziehungen,* vol. 4. no 1.

Schulten, T. (1998), 'Tarifpolitik unter den Bedingungen der Europäischen Währungsunion – Überlegungen zum Aufbau eines tarifpolitischen Mehr-Ebenen-Systems am Beispiel der westeuropäischen Metallindustrie', *WSI-Mitteilungen,* 7, pp. 482-493.

Schulten, T. (1998), 'Perspektiven nationaler Kollektivvertragsbeziehungen im integrierten Europa', in, Kohler-Koch, B. (ed)., *Regieren in entgrenzten Räumen,* PVS Sonderheft 29.

Sörries, B. (1998), 'Die Europäisierung von Arbeitsbeziehungen: Der soziale Dialog und seine Akteure. Eine empirische Untersuchung der Zentralebene sowie ausgewählter Sektoren', Mss., Constance.

Stöckl, I. (1986), *Gewerkschaftsausschüsse in der EG,* Kehl, Strassbourg, Arlington.

Streeck, W. (1998), 'The Internationalization of Industrial Relations in Europe: Prospects and Problems', MPIfG Discussion Paper 98/2, Cologne.

Streeck, W. and Vitols, S. (1993), 'European Works Councils: Between Statutory Enactment and Voluntary Adoption', Discussion Paper of the Wissenschaftszentrum Berlin, FS I 93-312, Berlin.

Traxler, F. (1995), 'Entwicklungstendenzen in den Arbeitsbeziehungen Westeuropas', in: Mesch, M. (ed.), *Sozialpartnerschaft und Arbeitsbeziehungen in Europa,* Vienna.

Traxler, F. (1996), 'European Trade Union Policy and Collective Bargaining – Mechanisms and Levels of Labour Market Regulation in Comparison', *Transfer,* 2, pp. 287-297.

Weyer, J. (1997), 'Weder Ordnung noch Chaos. Die Theorie sozialer Netzwerke zwischen Insitutionalismus und Selbstorganisationstheorie', in, Weyer, J. et. al., *Technik, die Gesellschaft schafft: soziale Netzwerke als Ort der Technikgenese*, Berlin.

*For Product Safety Concerns and Information please contact
our EU representative GPSR@taylorandfrancis.com Taylor & Francis
Verlag GmbH, Kaufingerstraße 24, 80331 München, Germany*

T - #0126 - 160425 - C0 - 219/153/9 - PB - 9781138702691 - Gloss Lamination